THE *Christian* LEADERSHIP DILEMMA

THE
Christian
LEADERSHIP
DILEMMA
How to Move Ahead with Grace
and Keep the Faith

F.D. Magnelli

NASHVILLE

NEW YORK • LONDON • MELBOURNE • VANCOUVER

THE *Christian* LEADERSHIP DILEMMA
How to Move Ahead with Grace *and* Keep the Faith

Published in New York, New York, by Morgan James Publishing. Morgan James is a trademark of Morgan James, LLC. www.MorganJamesPublishing.com

Proudly distributed by Ingram Publisher Services.

Unless otherwise noted, Scripture quotations are taken from the Holy Bible, King James Version (Public Domain).

Scripture quotations or phrases marked "ESV" are taken from the ESV® Bible (The Holy Bible, English Standard Version®), copyright © 2001 by Crossway, a publishing ministry of Good News Publishers. Used by permission. All rights reserved.

Morgan James BOGO™

A **FREE** ebook edition is available for you or a friend with the purchase of this print book.

_____

CLEARLY SIGN YOUR NAME ABOVE

Instructions to claim your free ebook edition:
1. Visit MorganJamesBOGO.com
2. Sign your name CLEARLY in the space above
3. Complete the form and submit a photo of this entire page
4. You or your friend can download the ebook to your preferred device

ISBN 978-1-63195-703-1 paperback
ISBN 978-1-63195-704-8 ebook
Library of Congress Control Number:
2021913580

Cover Design by:
Rachel Lopez
www.r2cdesign.com

Morgan James PUBLISHING Builds with... **Habitat for Humanity** Peninsula and Greater Williamsburg

Morgan James is a proud partner of Habitat for Humanity Peninsula and Greater Williamsburg. Partners in building since 2006.

Get involved today! Visit MorganJamesPublishing.com/giving-back

For all those courageous souls, some current and some in the past, who pursue the things of God and endeavor to spread the message of Christ.

CONTENTS

ACKNOWLEDGMENTS

My heart, soul, mind, and strength of love and thanks to my Heavenly Father, who, through my Lord Jesus Christ, has called me to serve the bread of life. Despite all my own shortcomings and human frailties, He still only sees the best in me.

My deepest and heartfelt love and thanks to my wife and partner, Robin, who has been a lifelong example to me of a holy and virtuous woman, and our son, Benji, who has a heart of gold for God and the courage to live it and share it. I thank them for their unwavering love and support on behalf of Christ to live and see this Word of God reach the hearts of those seeking.

My thanks also go to Michelle Cencich, Cathy Hobbs, Mark Moran, Gary Frederick, and Victoria Finley, who have each contributed in different ways to this project, such as typing, proofreading, editing, encouraging, and providing insightful commentary.

My gratitude extends to the team at Morgan James Publishing for taking my book into new places.

Finally, my humble recognition for all those courageous souls, some current and some in the past, who pursue the things of God and endeavor to spread the message of Christ and whose labors have provided insight, encouragement, and the scriptural tools to press forward. It is from these fellow workers' lives, hearts, and labors I have learned much and owe more. I thank these fellow laborers in the Lord, who no doubt at some personal cost to themselves, chose to follow God's guidance and lay aside their own comfort and ease in order to move ahead with grace and keep the faith. Their broad shoulders have provided me comfort and shade under the shadow of their efforts to labor myself in the master's field. My thanks to them for staying true to their God-inspired course even when facing a tide of obstacles. May they be rewarded by our Lord at his coming.

INTRODUCTION

Who then is Paul, and who is Apollos, but ministers by whom
ye believed, even as the Lord gave to every man? I have planted,
Apollos watered; but God gave the increase
(I Cor. 3:5–6).

God is the only one who can cause the life of His Word to grow in an individual, or a local church, or any Christian ministry. We labor together with Him, and then plant and water for a time. But it is He who causes the seed of the Word that is planted and watered in the heart of man to grow continuously through His grace. God always honors man's free will. Since the time of the early church leaders even to the present, God continues to work together with those who are willing to work with Him to further the knowledge of the gospel of grace regarding His Son, Jesus Christ. Good leaders are those, with or without titles, who take the initiative to move with God and set the pace and right moral example for others to follow. Such leaders are moral agents for Christ-like transformation from the heart that begins with themselves and then spreads to others.

Yet, we read in the pages of God's Word, and still witness today, resistance and even direct opposition to the furtherance of the gospel of His grace. At times this opposition, whether unwittingly or not, comes from a group we would never suspect—some Christian leaders. I am speaking of the Christian leaders who have forgotten their role as laborers together with God. When these leaders cross that line and resist the will of God, they become worldly and carnal in their thinking, and the grace of God becomes buried in myths and commandments of men. Many institutional and denominational monuments to men have been built upon these false foundations and ideas. These leaders navigate in a worldly or business model rather than a Word-based service one. Leaders fail when they resist God and turn to practices that glorify men. The Christian leadership dilemma has been and continues to be first and foremost a moral one of which Christ is the quintessential example to follow. God's way or the way of world is the choice.

Despite resistance, God through Christ reaches out to promote quality Christian living and fellowship to those who will listen. Such quality can only be built upon the right foundation of the truth of God's Word.

I Corinthians 3:9–11:

For we are labourers together with God: ye are God's husbandry, *ye are* God's building.

According to the grace of God which is given unto me, as a wise masterbuilder, I have laid the foundation, and another buildeth thereon. But let every man take heed how he buildeth thereupon.

For other foundation can no man lay than that is laid, which is Jesus Christ.

The Apostle Paul faced resistance and opposition from religious leaders when he moved with God as a laborer sharing the gospel of God's grace and the faith of Jesus Christ. When accused of criminal action and brought before the authority of that day, Paul responded as recorded in Acts 26.

Acts 26:1–2:

. . . Then Paul stretched forth the hand, and answered for himself:

I think myself happy, king Agrippa, because I shall answer for myself this day before thee touching all the things whereof I am accused of the Jews [Judeans].

The words "answered" in verse 1 and "answer" in verse 2 are translated from the Greek verb *apologeomai*, the root form of the word *apologia*. This word looks like the English word "apology" and the English synonym "apologia." The English word "apology" developed from this Greek word. Yet, an apology was not what Paul provided. He did not admit wrongdoing or guilt for his actions!

This word means "to defend oneself; make one's defense." However, this is no ordinary case. It deals with truth and error regarding God's only begotten Son, Jesus Christ, and what he came to accomplish on behalf of mankind.

How did Paul defend himself? Well, having knowledge of this Greek word is not enough to answer this question. We must seek the biblical meaning, as it is divinely used in the Holy Scriptures and specifically in this passage. As we do, a deeper meaning emerges, revealing what Paul communicated. Paul spoke truth in the face of accusation. Those accusing Paul were religious leaders of the day, steeped in the Judaic Law and their own works, unwilling to yield to God's direction of grace and the faith concerning Jesus Christ.

Paul was human like the rest of us. Even a child understands the hurt and damage caused by false accusations. How do you think Paul felt? Perhaps you or someone you know and love has faced such accusations. I have. It is not fun.

Leveling accusations against the innocent is not a new practice. It is an ancient tactic executed by morally bereft leaders to retain control of people and draw attention away from political and religious corruption. Such leaders have failed in their responsibility and privilege to serve. It is "by their fruit" that such leaders, and really everyone, should be known. "Fruit" is a figurative term for noticeable results that are produced from the effort or actions put into an endeavor. Fruit can be perceived and traced back to its cause or origin. What are people producing by their actions?

Matthew 12:33:

Either make the tree good, and his fruit good; or else make the tree corrupt, and his fruit corrupt: for the tree is known by *his* fruit.

It is not difficult to understand that a tree is known by its fruit, good or corrupt. It's no different with people. This simple analogy can help us during a conflict, when on the surface things may not be clear. How? By reading people's fruit, we discover one of the great keys to getting to the truth. When we as followers of Christ see things that do not appear to line up with God's Word, we need to dig below the surface. Identifying fruit and then tracing it back to the cause may take time. However, the fruit will eventually show itself, good or corrupt. That is the indicator we should seek.

Galatians 6:7–9:

Be not deceived; God is not mocked: for whatsoever a man soweth, that shall he also reap.

For he that soweth to his flesh shall of the flesh reap corruption; but he that soweth to the Spirit shall of the Spirit reap life everlasting.

And let us not be weary in well doing: for in due season we shall reap, if we faint not.

Planting something below the surface of the ground will eventually reveal a result. Such a simple analogy also works with people. What people have put in their hearts eventually shows itself as well. Those who sow to their flesh are sense-knowledge or natural-guided Christians whose walk is no longer guided by the spirit of God and the spiritual knowledge of His Word. Their efforts will eventually break the surface for all to see. Such activity may appear sincere, religious, and zealous. We should not be deceived, and we should remember that God is not mocked or fooled by appearances. He looks on the heart of man.

Surface thinking is a thief that often steals the reality of a matter. For example, if we live life relying only on appearances, we will miss some of the most wonderful experiences and people we may not have taken the time to know because of their appearance. It steals true understanding because often what lies beneath the surface is the true heart of a matter (". . . the truth shall make you free" John 8:32).

Reading fruit is so important, especially when it comes to leaders. If the fruit is good, wonderful. If the fruit is corrupt, then someone needs to speak up about it. People may start out with good fruit, and the struggle or system wears them down. Each situation may be different. Whether they start out or learn bad practice along the way is not the point here. What matters is when people with bad fruit gain positions of authority, their bad practices become amplified. Then corruption, accusation, and mistreatment of others will eventually follow and those impacted suffer.

Anyone who has faced these conditions can identify with Paul. And his example speaks loudly to us today. Despite all the accusations leveled at him, he moved ahead with grace, ". . . by the grace of God I am what I am . . . I laboured more abundantly than they all: yet not I, but the grace of God which was with me" (I Corinthians 15:10) and "kept the faith" (II Timothy 4:7).

In some ways, this book is dedicated to those courageous Christians who have and continue to stand against such a negative environment. It is intended to provide answers of truth in response to such attacks. It is a voice calling to us who truly desire to know how to navigate the Christian experience successfully in the wilderness of accusations.

It is the moral imperative of the church to set the pace and example for ethical behavior. The advancement of technology, though impressive, is not the moral compass from which to derive bearings. Society and its variety of disciplines (government, the press, business, education, entertainment, etc.) take their moral cues from the church. The importance of this dynamic between the church and society cannot be overstated.

The Christian Leadership Dilemma exposes static and decaying elements that have attached themselves to the Christian experience for years. Such decay starts when leaders fail to carry out their God-given privilege and responsibility and distinguish right from wrong in the moral sphere. This is the Christian leadership dilemma. When such elements are exposed, they are often met with resistance. The truths contained in this book will challenge the status quo or established order, particularly if that order does not rest squarely upon God's right foundation—Jesus Christ and his accomplished work.

Overview

This book is divided into five chapters. In the first chapter, we see that leaders are called to be true servants and helpers of the believers' joy. Further, they are moral examples who willingly teach and guide others in Christ. Leaders are not to lord over, or dominate, the believers by leveraging power to isolate and control them.

The second chapter discusses the believers' focus on God and His Word in overcoming any challenge. God and His Word are always right, which is the standpoint from which we can settle any issues among us.

The third chapter identifies how the believers are to respond to conflict, either from within the church or from without (spiritual attacks originate from either direction). As believers recognize and boldly respond to the Spirit's direction to us and in us, we move together in one accord, looking to God for solutions.

The fourth chapter explains "the ministry"—all individual and collective service and labor performed on behalf of Christ. And the distinction between the ministry and the household of faith.

In the final chapter, obedience to the household of faith is set as both starting point and standard to be maintained for the Christian believer. It is characterized by:

- Obeying God rather than men
- Standing upon our God-given justification through the faith of Jesus Christ
- Accepting only God as supreme judge
- Walking by the spirit
- Most significantly, obedience to the household of faith promotes a "respect came upon every soul" attitude (Acts 2:43), which is the first practical step in moving ahead with grace and keeping the faith. A mutually respectful environment encourages both—

individual growth and personal contribution of the spiritual strengths we all have to offer.

My encouragement to you is to allow the truth of this Word contained in this book to make you free, and God will illuminate your heart and guide your steps to move ahead with grace and keep the faith.

F.D. Magnelli, Melbourne, Florida, USA

Chapter 1

LEADERS ARE SERVANTS, HELPERS OF THE BELIEVERS' JOY, AND EXAMPLES

I t is vital to the life of a Christian community to have quality leaders. When these leaders work together with God, their efforts are prosperous, and the fruit of their labor is good. Good leaders are those, with or without titles, who take the initiative to move with God and retain a Christ-centered moral compass. In doing so, they are catalysts that set the spiritual pace and right moral example for others to follow.

God expects His people to work in unity with Him and not stray into their own pursuits outside of direction and inspiration from Him. God knows how to work with people and not overstep His boundaries. He does not control people or force their decisions. God always allows people to exercise freedom of will. The job of a godly leader is to treat people with respect and allow them the same freedom, but this is not always what happens within Christian groups today. When leaders overstep the freedom God affords all men, this is when leaders fail. Overtly or covertly manipulating the freedom of others is ethically wrong.

To unveil the correct lifestyle of a Christian leader, let's begin by looking at three biblical examples: Jesus Christ, the Apostle Paul, and the Apostle Peter. Each one, as shown in the Bible, denounced the practice of leaders lording over God's people. This practice is commonly known in secular circles as "top-down leadership."

Top-down leadership occurs in the absence of true service when someone imposes their will upon another through a position of leverage. This behavior oversteps a Christian leader's God-given role. It sets up a respect-of-persons hierarchy that undermines the Christian community. This does not mean leaders cannot have strong opinions or preferences, provided they are based on godly values. These viewpoints are to be voiced with mutual respect and consideration for the opinions and preferences of others who, likewise, hold the truth in high esteem.

Sometimes leaders cross this line and infringe on the free will of others by imposing their will on them. Compliance can momentarily pass as a success. But have they really succeeded to initiate a positive change for others that will last? Probably not.

Any parent knows this is possible when raising children. My wife helped me see this when our son was very young. She said, "You can force him to do something now because you are bigger than him but what happens when he is older? That approach will not work." This stopped me in my tracks and caused me to change. She encouraged me to positively guide him, which would produce better results as he grew into a man. She was right. Parenting and leadership involve very similar principles. Yet some might think working with adults is different. It isn't.

Let me say we all are fallible at times and may not always put forth our best efforts when we are tired or overcome amid challenges.

However, for Christian leaders, this must not become habitual. We need to get help if we have fallen into this pattern. If left unchecked, this overstep can fuel the temptation to lord over God's people.

Three Examples: Leaders of Leaders

As we will see, our three biblical examples, including the greatest leader of all time, speak volumes against this practice to all who have "eyes to see, and ears to hear."

First, Jesus Christ contrasted the practice of lording over people with the converse practice of humbly serving people. Service is the remedy to the ills of lording over people. Since the time Jesus declared his public ministry in his hometown of Nazareth, through washing the feet of his disciples on the night he was betrayed and eventually giving his life at Calvary right up to this very day, it is the right thing to do. Next, the Apostle Paul contrasted lording over God's people with being a helper of the believers' joy. Finally, the Apostle Peter contrasted being lords over God's people with being an example of willingly teaching and guiding others. In every one of these categories, it is incumbent for us to measure the quality of leaders by reading the fruit they produce and whether it lines up with the Word of God and godly values.

Each of these three examples builds one upon another and is mutually inclusive. In other words, the comprehensive picture of leadership includes all three essential elements blended together harmoniously.

Lording over people is a common occurrence by worldly standards. Either an explicit or implied hierarchy, or "pecking order," often guides leadership activity in organizations. There is a place for decisive and more focused leadership, especially during a crisis. Yet true leadership is not about a top-down, or corporate-ladder, mentality.

Most people who have worked in such settings understand how knowledge and position are used to leverage advantage over others. This leadership approach culminates in elevating the one who leverages to their advantage more skillfully. As a result, people are used as stepping-stones, rungs on the ladder of personal success, rather than collective success. Personal success at the expense of collective success is not the approach to leadership taught and endorsed by Jesus Christ.

Jesus Christ: The Perfect Servant

On the night of his last supper before being taken by the religious authorities, when he taught his disciples that bread and wine would be a remembrance of his broken body and shed blood, Jesus Christ confronted the wrong approach to leading. Then he gave them the right perspective—service.

Luke 22:24–25:

And there was also a strife among them [the leaders present], which of them should be accounted the greatest.

And he [Jesus] said unto them, The kings [leaders] of the Gentiles [not Israel] exercise lordship over them; and they that exercise authority upon them are called benefactors.

The apostles argued among themselves, saying, "Who is the greatest?" If left unchecked, this attitude would set up a hierarchy or pyramid in which one person is logically above another. This approach was not what Jesus endeavored to teach them about true leadership. So, he addressed this worldly attitude by providing the key ingredient of true leadership—a heart of service.

Luke 22:26–27:

But ye *shall* not be so [it couldn't be any clearer]: but he that is greatest among you, let him be as the younger; and he that is chief, as he that doth serve.

For whether is greater, he that sitteth at meat, or he that serveth? is not he that sitteth at meat? but I am among you as he that serveth.

Jesus Christ made a clear and unmistakable assessment of leadership. Worldly leaders want to be served more than to serve others. This dispute among the apostles on "who would be the greatest" is the world's definition of leadership—not God's.

We see examples of rankings and hierarchies in many competitions. Who is the greatest Olympian? What is the greatest team that ever won the World Series or the Super Bowl? Who is the greatest player of all time? What is the best movie of the year at the Oscars? Or the best actor or the best screenplay? It's all about the best, the best, the best! I may enjoy these competitions for entertainment, but they do not set the right example of Christian leadership. What a wake-up call! This is the way of the world. And when this happens among Christian leaders, problems follow.

Healthy competition and striving for excellence are noble pursuits if they also help to shape good character. Competition without comparison is achievable within a team atmosphere. Comparison defeats the idea of a team. On a real team, each member truly desires to bring out the best in one another. The idea of equal in importance but not equal in function is at the core of a team. The type of comparison that breeds strife can be an unquenchable fire that consumes the best of intentions. The spiritual leader is not in competition with other leaders because this is not wise.

II Corinthians 10:12:
For we dare not make ourselves of the number, or compare ourselves with some that commend themselves: but they

measuring themselves by themselves, and comparing themselves among themselves, are not wise.

In Luke 22:25, the words "exercise lordship over" are the one Greek word *kurieuō*. It means "to be lord over any person or anything, to have dominion over." Things are to be used but people are to be loved, and we should never mix up the two. When we do, we have removed ourselves from God's heart of love and are not walking according to His Word. God is love and always loves, so no wonder people are so precious to Him. We use material things, and if they break, we decide whether to throw them away. But we do not "throw away" people.

However, there are times when we may believe that people's bad behavior warrants the need to excuse ourselves from their company. This is a personal decision to limit our relationship with them because we mutually disagree on biblical behavior. In these cases, bringing this to their attention and redefining the parameters of the relationship may be in order to keep the peace.

II Thessalonians 3:14–16:

And if any man obey not our word by this epistle, note that man, and have no company with *him*, that he may be ashamed.[1]

Yet count him not as an enemy, but admonish [warn, in ESV] him as a brother.

Now the Lord of peace himself give you peace always by all means. The Lord *be* with you all.

Christian Ministries Today

In our modern culture, Christian ministries can be large organizations that require structure in order to distribute responsibilities and organize

---

1   "To have an innate moral repugnance to the doing of a dishonorable act." (See endnotes under Ethelbert W. Bullinger)

activities. These structures should be made with good stewardship and the best utilization of resources in mind. There may be two sides to this—a corporate or business side and a biblical side. How can the two be compatible yet not competitive or combative? The biblical side of the organization must focus on teaching and ministering the Word of God.

The corporate or business side is designed to steward physical resources (e.g., employee salaries, buildings, books, and travel). The business side must always be subordinate to the biblical side of the ministry. The teaching and advancement of the Word of God must always come first.

It is important to help people understand the importance of keeping priorities clear in running any Christian activity or organization. Elevating and maintaining God's Word first above the business side of a ministry is a great key to keep God involved in the work. (Matthew 6:33: But seek ye first the kingdom of God, and His righteousness; and all these things shall be added unto you.) When the Word is not first, God is not first, which inherently leads to idolatry in some form. This pattern results in people being treated poorly, causing hurt and confusion.

When people are treated as if they are physical things that can be manipulated, used, and discarded, that is a result of worldly influence. When an imbalance exists with a top-down leadership approach, rather than a balanced biblical approach among leaders, there is a problem. Consequently, there is a disconnect between the leadership and people who genuinely desire to serve on behalf of Christ. Mutual belief in God and spiritual unity get interrupted. That is exactly what Jesus Christ warned his leaders against.

A Christian ministry that uses a pyramid leadership design that can leverage advantage—the base being the believers and the pinnacle being the concentration of authority at the top—does not work well. Incorporating more of the Body-of-Christ approach or team approach yields the best results. The latter environment is where spiritual strengths function and there is healthy two-way communication. Everyone is responsible for their own life decisions. Ephesians Chapter 4 presents a biblical approach in which a Christian ministry maintains an environment where all believers contribute and benefit from service in Christ. This environment is the aim of organizing on behalf of Christ.

Ephesians 4:11–16:

And he gave some, apostles; and some, prophets; and some, evangelists; and some, pastors and teachers [gifts of service given to the church].

For the perfecting of the saints, for the work of the ministry, for the edifying of the body of Christ:

Till we all come in the unity of the [household of] faith, and of the knowledge of the Son of God, unto a perfect man, unto the measure of the stature of the fulness of Christ:

That we *henceforth* be no more children [in spiritual understanding, not in age], tossed to and fro, and carried about with every wind of doctrine, by the sleight of men, *and* cunning craftiness, whereby they lie in wait to deceive;

But speaking the truth in love, may grow up into him in all things, which is the head, *even* Christ:

From whom the whole body fitly joined together and compacted by that which every joint supplieth, according to the effectual working in the measure of every part, maketh increase of the body unto the edifying of itself in love.

The Body-of-Christ model shows how to successfully build a team of Christian believers that actively makes room for and, indeed, encourages people to contribute according to their desires and commensurate with their spiritual strengths. Such a team is a God-inspired living example of spiritual unity. This approach requires humility, listening, and willingness to work together. A Christian ministry is like a vehicle that can transport and move the truth to those who hunger and thirst after righteousness. It is not an end in itself. Its goal is not to simply perpetuate itself. It exists to serve others.

Spiritual unity is maintained as we hold ourselves upright to each other in love. We are accountable to each other. This is done through genuine humility, gentleness, and patience. The result is the true bond of peace among us.

Ephesians 4:1–3

I therefore, the prisoner of the Lord, beseech you that ye walk worthy of the vocation wherewith ye are called,

With all lowliness and meekness, with longsuffering, forbearing one another in love;

Endeavouring to keep the unity of the Spirit in the bond of peace.

The Apostle Paul: Helper of Their Joy

Jesus Christ said the remedy to lording over people was service. Now we will look at Paul's antidote to the malady of lording over others. With each broad stroke added, the clear portrait of spiritual leadership emerges. Paul notes the unhealthy practice of lording over people is to be countered with being helpers of the believers' joy.

II Corinthians 1:24:

Not for that we have dominion over [Greek word *kurieuō*] your [the] faith [of Jesus Christ], but are helpers of your joy: for by [the] faith [of Jesus Christ], ye stand [Greek verb *estēkate*].[2]

---

2   *estēkate* from *histēmi* and means here the standing action occurs in the past with its effect or completion in present. This is in reference to the enduring impact of the new birth and receiving the faith of Jesus Christ.

In this Scripture, the Apostle Paul and his protégé Timothy said they did not have dominion over the faith of Jesus Christ that each individual is given at the new birth. The faith of Jesus Christ is his accomplished work we all share as brothers and sisters in the family of God. Instead, they were helpers, working alongside people where they were in their walks and lives so they could have joy. The words "have dominion over" are translated from the same Greek word *kurieuō* as in Luke 22:25, where it is translated as "exercise lordship over." In contrast, here we see that leaders are to be helpers of the believers' joy. This is where a real understanding of free will comes into play for the Christian leader.

Dominion over others is about controlling people. We control things, but we never control people. There is nothing wrong with being in charge of yourself and a situation. Jesus Christ was a master at this; he was in charge of himself, and he was in charge of every situation, as the four gospels (Matthew, Mark, Luke, and John) clearly show. But leaders are not authorized to be in control of people; they do not have dominion over others' faith and what they do with it. This is profoundly important to distinguish and understand.

Thomas Jefferson, the third President of the United States, declared, "I have sworn upon the altar of God eternal hostility against every form of tyranny over the mind of man." Free will is something very sacred to protect. However, free will is not the right to violate other people or existing laws.

Christian leaders are to teach, and then allow people to make up their own minds. Intervention has its place as well. When someone is a danger to themselves or others, this requires action, but it should not be the norm.

Inspiring and encouraging people to love God, believe His Word, and love themselves as well as others is a profitable, noble endeavor. This endeavor can be challenging because people often make mistakes, either by their own ignorance, carelessness, or stubbornness, even when they are lovingly warned. Christian leaders who are sound in the doctrine must patiently continue to teach the Word, aiming for joy in the lives of others as they learn to stand strong. Joy is a fruit of the spirit, and it indicates quality of life. We want quality and stability in the lives of God's people. It is never to be about controlling people.

Galatians 4:16–17:

Am I therefore become your enemy, because I tell you the truth? [Paul's asking the Galatians because I tell you the truth, does that mean I am your enemy? No! We are supposed to speak the truth.]

They zealously affect you, *but* not well; yea, they would exclude you, that ye might affect them.

This is somewhat of an awkward translation. In the Amplified Bible, verse 17 reads, *These men [the Judaizing teachers] are zealously trying to dazzle you—paying court to you, making much of you; but their purpose is not honorable or worthy or for any good. What they want to do is to isolate you [from us who oppose them], so that they may win you over to their side and get you to court their favor.*

Isolating and controlling people in order to secure their allegiance is a carnal, natural knowledge approach to leadership. This tactic is often infested with favors and flattery. And when these tactics do not work, then intimidation and fear are the tools of domineering leaders. Either way, some sort of bondage or obligation always follows. These tactics form the psychological bars that encase people in mental prisons. Only truth releases people from being imprisoned in their own mind (John 8:32).

II Corinthians 1:24:

Not for that we have dominion over your [the] faith [of Jesus Christ], but are helpers of your joy: for by [the] faith [of Jesus Christ] ye stand [Greek verb *estēkate*].

Paul contrasts the practice of exercising dominion over people's faith in Jesus Christ with being helpers of others' joy. The faith of Jesus Christ is all about the grace of God and not one's own works. Paul is saying his aim, in contrast to "lording over," is to help others build on this foundation of grace.

Leaders who fall prey to the temptation of dominating other people usually have titles and assets to protect. That is the wrong approach. We must win, not coerce, people. From the youngest to the oldest and from the novice to the veteran Christian believer. We win people to Jesus Christ (II Corinthians 4:5), not to ourselves. We win them to God's team, not to the ranks or roster of any group or organization.

We see in this verse the service of leaders, how Paul worked with people, rather than by pressuring them. "Helpers" in verse 24 is the Greek word *sunergos*, translated "fellow worker, work fellow, fellow labourer, labourer together with, companion in labour, fellow helper, helper."

E.W. Bullinger's lexicon defines this word as "working together in conjunction with." Paul labored with them, not against them.

The lording over approach of leadership is not a *do-it-together* transformational approach where everyone benefits but a *use-you-to-benefit-me* transaction, which often results in winners and losers. Such a transactional "exchanging one thing for another" approach does not really help people. Rather a transformational approach is ideal. It involves a greater investment in the individual to draw out the best in others that inspires "mutual stimulation and elevation that converts followers into leaders and may convert leaders into moral agents," as

James Macgregor Burns notes and further elaborates in his book on leadership. Burns cogently captures in contemporary terminology what we are seeing about how the Apostle Paul engaged with others. It is worth noting that the vital and constructive concepts of leadership as well as their antitheses are all found in the Bible.

It was the last day before the holiday break. My first-grade teacher, Mrs. Bell, noticed I was having difficulty completing my assigned worksheet. Completion of the worksheet was required before coloring my holiday decoration to bring home to hang on our tree. Everyone had finished theirs and were gone, and I was left alone feeling the pressure. She came over and gently accepted my worksheet at the point where I was and allowed me to color my holiday ornament.

I have remembered this simple act of kindness my whole life. Why? She worked with me where I was. This was transformational for me and has helped me to understand how to work with people. God works with us in a similar way, right where we are at the time. We certainly can do this for others.

A great key in working with people is to start right where they are. Waiting for perfection in people is not a viable approach. Everyone comes with a background. Loving patience, tender care, and encouragement can go a long way in helping others. There must also be teaching involved that instructs in a better way, God's way, than perhaps people might have been aware of or chosen up to that point.

It takes effort to work with people side-by-side to help them develop a lifestyle of joy. This joy comes from recognizing we build quality Christian lives on the work of Jesus Christ, not on our own works. This labor that builds upon the work of Christ involves patience and care. It takes time to be with people in all different scenarios when they are challenged and when they celebrate (I Corinthians 12:26).

The needs of others may not always coincide with a leader's schedule. Therefore, such service and time spent with people may sometimes seem inconvenient. But the building process of wholeness can be measured one meaningful conversation, one heartfelt embrace, one willing and patient ear, one shoulder to lean on, and one fitly spoken word at a time. Such exchanges build genuine bonds and friendships that can last a lifetime. How valuable is that!

Joy is independent of circumstance and, therefore, can be found in the highs and lows of life that each of us has experienced. Joy is an expression of victory that can be realized despite any circumstance. This was evidenced by Jesus Christ himself while suffering for our sins on the cross (Hebrews 12:2). The labor of working with people to help them increase their joy, regardless of the ebb and flow of life, is part of the service a true leader provides. The Apostle Paul understood these truths. I look forward to meeting him someday.

The Apostle Peter: An Example to the Flock

Now let's look at the Apostle Peter. Remember, things are to be used and people are to be *loved*. It is not the other way around. This section specifically admonishes leaders to selflessly care for people while not lording authority over them. For this type of service, God promises there are future rewards.

I Peter 5:1–3:

The elders which are among you I exhort, who am also an elder, and a witness of the sufferings of Christ, and also a partaker of the glory that shall be revealed:

Feed the flock of God which is among you, taking the oversight *thereof*, not by constraint, but willingly; not for filthy lucre, but of a ready mind;

Neither as being lords over [*katakurieuō*] *God's* heritage, but being ensamples [examples] to the flock.

Here "being lords over" is from the same Greek word as "we have dominion over" in II Corinthians 1:24 and Luke 22:25. But it also has another word in front of it. Just like in English, in Greek, two words may be combined to become a compound word. The word *kata* in front of and joined to the word *kurieuō* adds intensity to the idea of not lording over. This compound word means "to hold in subjection, to be master of." That's very powerful!

In contrast, leaders are to be "ensamples," which is King James English for "examples." The Greek word for "ensamples" here means "an impression." It is like a hard object making an imprint on a softer surface. Leaders are to be examples to the end of making a good impression, making a godly imprint in word and deed on others. The best example of a leader is one whose actions line up with their words.[3]

Leadership is about service. Its aim is to promote joy, and it must be easy to follow so that the words spoken line up with actions taken. When actions do not follow words, this is perceived as hypocrisy, and the wrong impression is made. People should not follow bad imprints made by hypocritical leaders.

Matthew 23:1–4:
> Then spake Jesus to the multitude, and to his disciples,
> Saying, The scribes and the Pharisees sit in Moses' seat:
> All therefore whatsoever they bid you observe, *that* observe and do; but do not ye after their works: for they say, and do not.
> For they bind heavy burdens and grievous to be borne, and lay *them* on men's shoulders; but they *themselves* will not move them with one of their fingers.

---

3   Acts 1:1: "The former treatise have I made, O Theophilus, of all that Jesus began both to do and teach. . . ." Jesus Christ practiced what he preached, he did and taught, so his message was easy to follow.

Jesus Christ clearly exposed the scribes and Pharisees who sat in authority supposing to represent Moses. He warned the people not to follow the example of the scribes and Pharisees because they said one thing and did another. They would not do the very things they insisted others do. This is hypocrisy. Jesus Christ plainly warned against this practice when he pointed out to his disciples, "Beware ye of the leaven of the Pharisees, which is hypocrisy." (Luke 12:1) Just as a small amount of fermented dough (leaven) affects the whole lump of dough, so too hypocrisy grows and permeates everything it touches.

As we consider the context of being an example in I Peter 5:2, making that right impression so others can easily follow, we find deep truths revealed. Peter wrote, "Feed the flock of God which is among you, taking the oversight *thereof,* not by constraint, but willingly; not for filthy lucre, but of a ready mind . . ." Let us briefly consider these.

"Feed" here is a figurative reference to the whole array of duties and office of a shepherd. This includes not just feeding, but also leading, guiding, guarding, and encompassing the sheep for protection.

God's people are not literally sheep, and leaders are not really shepherds. But this illustration really helps us understand the care involved.

Leaders take on this responsibility and privilege willingly. They are not forced into it. Such spiritual oversight is not done for "filthy lucre" or dishonorable gain, it is not about the money, but with a "ready mind" or an eagerness and zeal. A leader is to be an example in motive. This starts with the purity and honesty each leader has before God which produces a whole person. Such wholeness is evidenced in living in the moment with satisfaction in Christ unhindered by the chains of the past or the anxieties of the future. The leader's wholeness—identity in Christ, maturity in Christ, and stand in Christ—is the core quality from which others will benefit from their example (I Timothy 4:16).

I Peter 5:4:
And when the chief Shepherd shall appear, ye shall receive a crown of glory that fadeth not away.

What awaits those who willingly embrace the care for God's people as noted here is a crown of glory. This crown is an eternal reward that will never fade. It is a benefit recognized and to be enjoyed unceasingly for such service rendered in love. It is perhaps not possible to overstate the magnitude of such a precious proposition straight from the heart of God Himself. Such truth provides deep insight into His perspective of those who genuinely and willingly care for His people. God notes and rewards sound moral character. How revealing this truly is!

As we have seen from Jesus Christ and the Apostle Paul and the Apostle Peter, leaders are not to lord over God's people. God has given Christian leaders authority, but only to the end of service. They are to be fellow workers with God's people with the aim of assisting them in joy and stability. They are to be examples in word, deed, and motive for others to follow.

Romans 13

An often-misunderstood section of Scripture regarding leaders can be found in the Book of Romans, Chapter 13. Rather than *governmental* authorities, as some suggest, these higher powers refer to *spiritual* leaders in the church, the Body of Christ, not anything organized by man.

Romans 13:1:
Let every soul be subject unto the higher powers [authorities]. For there is no power but of God: the powers that be are ordained of God.

The "higher powers" are not higher in terms of comparative elevation. In other words, this is not a hierarchy or pyramid approach to leadership in which the leaders are somehow in a lofty position above others. This would contradict what we just learned. These authorities are ministers given as gifts to serve others (e.g., Ephesians 4:8 and 11).

The "higher" is the *direction* from which that authority comes. These "higher powers" are "of God . . . ordained of God." The authority comes from heaven simply to facilitate service by teaching, guiding, and modeling what is right, so others can benefit.

In addition, there is no indication that this authority should be applied to any man-made structure. In other words, having a position or title in an organization does not mean that a person is a "higher power" from God's point of view. "Higher powers" are men or women God calls and gives authority to function in a unique role as a gift of service in the church.

Organizations appoint people to carry out responsibilities with access to people. If someone who is appointed also has such a calling from God, then there is a special benefit of service from God to people. The more responsibility one has, the greater the access and influence possible. However, a change in responsibility does not alter spiritual functioning in the Body of Christ.[4]

When a person moves from one organizationally appointed responsibility to another, there is no change in their spiritual calling. But changing a responsibility does change the amount of access and influence they have based on that responsibility. Paul and Peter were apostles wherever they went. Whether they were accepted as such is another matter entirely. Likewise, today "the gifts and calling of God are

---

4   Functioning in the Body of Christ refers to the interdependent role
    Christians perform as members in the church—Body of Christ, much like the
    interdependent roles members of the human body perform, e.g., eyes, legs, lungs,
    heart, spine, etc.

without repentance" (Romans 11:29), and everyone who serves adapts to the responsibilities wherever they go.

Spiritual calling to function and organizationally appointed positions should not be misconstrued to mean the same thing. They are not.

For example, an apostle, prophet, evangelist, pastor, or teacher can serve as such, whether they are in a rural area or in a city, or whether they serve at the forefront of the activity or behind the scenes. Through the highways and byways of life, in the United States or in other countries, they simply function according to God's calling.

Changes in organizational titles and positions occur when there is a reassignment of job or location, but these do not alter the gifts of God's grace. The variety of these gifts of grace are distributed by the Spirit (I Corinthians 12:4), meaning God Himself is involved. That is why these spiritual roles of service do not change based on any organizational realignment of man. If someone has a gift to the church of being a pastor, for example, that gift does not change because they move to a different location on the map . . . or because they have access to fewer people . . . or they are demoted by men to a position with fewer responsibilities in an organization.

Bold to Speak Up

When leaders at the top of a hierarchy brush aside venerable leaders and believers, then the practice of lording over God's people is most likely at work. This may happen because those leaders and/or believers have resisted the top-down leadership. Often, false accusations are leveled at those who speak up by those trying to preserve their control. The fruit of someone's walk is evident when God's Word is the standard. Yet, if accusation and intimidation rule above the standard of the Word, even the cry of common sense—awareness or judgments widely accepted as obviously practical and reasonable, goes unnoticed. The value of someone's opinion, even so-called "experts" in any field, can only be measured in direct proportion to their level of common sense. It is not right to assert that something is normal or biblical when the opposite is so strikingly obvious.

The Hans Christian Andersen tale, *The Emperor's New Clothes*, provides an interesting illustration. Andersen told a story of an emperor tricked by two charlatans. They convinced the emperor they could weave clothes for him that had astonishing quality—the clothes were invisible to those unfit to serve in their position or anyone that was a fool.

So, the entire kingdom was too intimidated to speak up about the emperor's obvious nakedness and pretended to see clothes that were not there. Consequently, because no one wanted to be labeled unfit or a fool, they pretended to admire the emperor's imaginary clothing that really did not exist. It wasn't until the emperor paraded his "new clothes" in public that a child spoke out and declared the emperor was not wearing anything. The emperor and his nobles continued to persist in the charade despite the whole town voicing the obvious—he was naked. The innocence of common sense awakened the rest. Common sense is a great weapon against groupthink, intimidation, and fear. What a revealing story. It shows what fear can do to people if left unchecked and unchallenged.

When believers see leaders lording over God's people, they all have the responsibility to speak up and expose the problem. Christian leaders should serve, being fellow workers of the believers' joy, and being good examples for others to follow. When God's Word mentions something once, that should be enough for God's people to pay attention. Yet, how compelling is it that we see Jesus Christ *and* the Apostle Paul *and* the Apostle Peter all make essentially the same point regarding leaders?

With such scriptural backup, you think it would be quite simple to correct, right? Well, sometimes such behavior is so subtle that it goes undetected or ignored for many years. But, more often than not, what really stops people from speaking up and standing up against intimidation is fear—fear of social media attacks or any such means of retribution, fear of being ostracized, fear of losing a job, or fear of losing standing in a group or community.

II Timothy 1:7:
> For God hath not given us the spirit of fear; but of power, and of love, and of a sound mind.

Fear is no way to live! Fear torments (I John 4:18). Certainly, fear at times has stopped each of us in our tracks. So, there is very little room for any of us to be accusatory or judgmental of anyone else. Yet, like the illustration of the child in the emperor's kingdom, there must come a time when we simply decide to be bold and speak up. It is to these bold souls to whom this book is dedicated. Speaking up and taking a stand on what is right doesn't mean we are harsh with people. We do it with love and tenderness, yet we are firm.

May Ephesians 6:19 and 20 be spoken of every one of us who do so.

> *And for me, that utterance may be given unto me, that I may open my mouth boldly, to make known the mystery of the gospel [good news regarding our identity in Christ and our relationship with one another in the household of faith and Body of Christ], For which I am an ambassador in bonds: that therein I may speak boldly, as I ought to speak.*

Chapter 2

GOD AND HIS WORD ARE RIGHT

How do we deal with disagreement and conflict among Christian believers? How do we proceed when there appears to be an impasse? Do we argue about who is right? Do we delve into *Whose side are you on?* Certainly, it is okay to have opinions on opinion topics, but if God declares something, it is no longer an opinion topic. It now becomes truth and is the final word on whatever category we happen to be discussing. So, when we stand with God on His Word, everything else tends to sort itself out.

When we as believers reach an impasse among ourselves, the question should not be who is right, but what is right. "Who is right?" or "Who do you stand or align yourself with?" leads us to focus on people and can fuel division. The correct response is "God and His Word are right" and "I stand with God and what He says is right." The impasse becomes less difficult to move forward from when the light of the Word is introduced into the situation.

Psalm 119:105:

Thy word *is* a lamp unto my feet, and a light unto my path.

It's the Word of God that allows us to navigate life successfully, avoiding unnecessary obstacles. It alone has the illuminating power, the light bright enough to expose even the subtlest of stumbling blocks.

Hebrews 4:12:

For the word of God *is* quick, and powerful, and sharper than any two-edged sword, piercing even to the dividing asunder of soul and spirit, and of the joints and marrow, and is a discerner of the thoughts and intents of the heart.

God's Word is quick and powerful, or "living and active." It's a living Word that is active, having a powerful edge to separate soul and spirit and the issues that proceed out of a person's heart. It reveals distinctions in life that are difficult to detect. For example, it can expose when evil has parasitically attached itself to good things, living off truth and even disguising itself as truth. Mature Christians, those who have learned to walk in love, light, and spiritual wisdom, need to recognize these distinctions and help others do the same.

Maturity in Christ is aided by "rightly dividing the word of truth" to the end we believe in the accomplished work of Christ (II Timothy 2:15). Our labor in the Word is not an academic or meritorious pursuit seeking God's approval. Neither is it to prove who we are in Christ to others. As Timothy was encouraged to do at a challenging time in the early years of the furtherance of the gospel, our diligence is to prove who we are in Christ to ourselves and that we are already approved through Christ to be in God's presence. This truth causes great freedom. Our diligence to rightly divide the word of truth is to fuel our own personal conviction that God has already accepted us through the work of Christ. God is not setting before us a scholarly challenge to receive His acceptance. This would be works not grace. Deeply considering and meditating upon the truth we discover is an aid to promote experiential knowledge of grace which puts us in the best position to detect subtle deceptions.

As a parent and schoolteacher, I have had many opportunities to observe children. Often, they make decisions based on whether they like or do not like something. As they mature and build strong moral character, they begin to make decisions based on what is right and what is wrong. This is similar to the Christian walk.

As we mature, we also move from the "milk" of the Word to the "meat." Metaphorically, milk is used to represent quite simple truths that can be taught to those just starting to learn the Word. If mature believers regress to a diet of milk, then their understanding becomes dull. They are unable to separate truth from error and good from evil.

Hebrews 5:12–14:

For when for the time ye ought to be teachers, ye have need that one teach you again which *be* the first principles of the oracles of God; and are become such as have need of milk, and not of strong meat.

For every one that useth milk *is* unskillful [inexperienced] in the word of righteousness: for he is a babe.

But strong meat belongeth to them that are of full age [mature], *even* those who by reason of use have their senses exercised to discern both good and evil.

The meat of the Word brings us beyond surface observations in life and into the realm of spiritual matters or "the deep things of God" (I Corinthians 2:10). Spiritual matters, or the deep things of God, are not discovered by the five senses or natural knowledge. Only spiritual knowledge and spiritual wisdom reveal the true condition of matters.

When looking at the surface of a snow-covered pond, it is difficult to know if it can support your weight. You must determine how thick the ice is before knowing the true condition of the pond. Likewise, with spiritual matters, you must look beyond the surface of matters.

For many people, this deeper perspective often goes unseen. But we cannot afford to be "surface thinkers" and expect to detect such subtleties. The deep things of God require time and patience to consider with unemotional detachment. In leadership as well as in all matters of life, we cannot give allegiance to a particular organizational position or title or what may appear as the face value of any matter and expect to have a clear understanding. We must look deeper. The Word of God provides us the most powerful tool available to accomplish a deeper dive into any matter.

The words translated "good" and "evil" in verse 14 are interesting when viewed from the Greek. They highlight why the meat of the Word is needed. For the sake of making this point, these words are left in their Greek characters here. The word "good" is translated from the Greek word καλοῦ and "evil" from the word κακοῦ. You do not need to know the Greek alphabet to notice there is only a one-character difference between the two words.

These two words look similar and even sound similar when spoken. When spoken, they rhyme (pronounced *ka-lōō* and *ka-kōō*). This is the figure of speech paronomasia, which draws attention to how similar sounding two words can be, yet they are miles apart in meaning. The worldly practices of lording over God's people or top-down leadership, as noted in Chapter 1, are often this subtle because they are veiled in platitudes, favors, and misdirection.

To illustrate the distinction between good and evil, we will consider two sections of the Book of Acts involving leadership. The first one exhibits how good fruit is produced when leaders follow the Word of God and His guidance. The second demonstrates what happens when religion and manmade forms of worship are followed. The first produced positive results with God; the second produced negative results with men. As biblical learners, we see that God often uses contrasts in His Word to help us understand certain truths—like light versus darkness and works of the flesh versus fruit of the spirit. When juxtaposed, these contrasts highlight one another, making distinctions easier to recognize.

Acts 15: God's Grace Is Right

The first example is in Acts 15, where the apostles were together as a group while contemplating and discussing a course of action in response to a challenge in the early church. The action that ensued helped the Word move dynamically forward to reach others. The second example is in Acts 21 when the apostles were not together as a group. The action taken here resulted in the Word not moving forward. The knowledge of God's grace was brushed aside and replaced by the works of men. First, let us see Acts 15.

Acts 15:1–2:

And certain men which came down from Judaea taught the brethren, *and* said, Except ye be circumcised[5] after the manner of Moses, ye cannot be saved.

---

5   Circumcision is a sign of an agreement with God as noted here: "Circumcision embodies and applies [the] covenant [agreement] promises and summons to a life of covenant obedience...which God makes of those whom he calls to himself and marks with the sign of his covenant." (See endnotes under J.D. Douglas, et. al.)

When therefore Paul and Barnabas had no small dissension and disputation with them, they determined that Paul and Barnabas, and certain other of them, should go up to Jerusalem unto the apostles and elders about this question.

Religious Judeans who were still zealous for the Law of Moses came from Judea to Antioch where there was a thriving Christian community. These legal zealots stirred up trouble by insisting that salvation required the work of circumcision according to Judean Law—meaning performing a physical act to enter into an agreement with God through obedience and gain the benefits of His promises.

The phrase "apostles and elders" comes up five times in this fifteenth chapter (verses 2, 4, 6, 22, and 23). The reiteration of this phrase is significant in understanding this section, and its absence in the next section (Acts 21) speaks loudly. Those who earnestly desire to know truth can see these details while reading the Scriptures.

Acts 15:3–4:

And being brought on their way by the church, they passed through Phenice and Samaria, declaring the conversion of the Gentiles: and they caused great joy unto all the brethren.

And when they were come to Jerusalem, they were received of the church, and *of* the apostles and elders, and they declared all things that God had done with them.

There was "great joy" among the brothers and sisters in Christ regarding others getting born again and receiving the gift of holy spirit. They declared what God had done "with" them. It wasn't "about" them. It was about what God was doing. When we get excited about what God is doing in our lives and communities and fellowships, we want to tell people.

The key word here is "with" in verse 4. It is translated from the Greek preposition *meta*, which can be rendered "together with . . . on the same side or party with." The sense of doing things with God, being on His side, or in association with God comes through in meaning. We can call it partnering with God or sharing together with Him in fellowship. This is what God really wants.

God is more interested in what we do *with* Him than anything we do *for* Him. Doing things with God implies a partnership and relationship with Him. Prayer and godly expectations (Ephesians Chapters 1–3) are part of this process.

On the other hand, doing things *for* God can often turn into a personal crusade that excludes God and His righteousness to gain our own righteousness (Romans 10:3). The example of the medieval campaigns comes to mind, better known as the "Crusades". These crusades were on a grander scale than any personal ones and loom large on the stage of history as a stain on the backdrop of Christianity. They were forged by religious zealots and opportunists "in the name of God" which had little if anything to do with God and more to do with political and personal agendas.

We must be careful when doing things for God that we do not allow those actions to turn into works to be accepted *by* God. Good works proceed from the spirit in us and are what we do when we partner with God via grace (II Corinthians 9:8). In contrast, works are what we do without God and are rooted in the flesh and not the spirit (Galatians 5:19–23). We can perform good works because of knowing God's love and grace, not works in order to be accepted by Him. Seeking such acceptance also leads to seeking acceptance from men. We have already been accepted by His grace in the beloved (Ephesians 1:6) through Jesus Christ.

God wants to be involved in our lives. He is the one who opens the eyes of our understanding heart to His light ("...the eyes of your hearts enlightened, that you may know…." Ephesians 1:18, ESV) as He is light (I John 1:5) and the Father of lights (James 1:17). He is the one who brings us comfort as the God of all comfort (II Corinthians 1:3). He is the one who brings peace into our hearts as the God of peace (Romans 15:33; 16:20). He is the one who provides the guidance and wisdom we need (Proverbs 3:5 and 6; James 3:17).

Acts 15:5–9:

But there rose up certain of the sect of the Pharisees which believed, saying, That it was needful to circumcise them, and to command *them* to keep the law of Moses.

And the apostles and elders came together for to consider of this matter.

And when there had been much disputing, Peter rose up, and said unto them, Men and brethren, ye know how that a good while ago God made choice among us, that the Gentiles by my mouth should hear the word of the gospel, and believe.

And God, which knoweth the hearts, bare them witness, giving them the Holy Ghost, even as *he did* unto us;

And put no difference between us and them, purifying their hearts by faith [the faith of Jesus Christ].

This issue was considered. There was disputing, and multiple participants had input. Including the right stakeholders in the discussion was important and is what led to the solution. This includes individuals with specific insight, even opposing viewpoints, and, of course, spiritual strengths that help to shape and mold the outcome.

In Christ, we are all equal. No one is above another, and no one is below. We all have Christ within us, and we share the same measure of faith (Romans 12:3). The household of faith means we share the common faith of Jesus Christ as brothers and sisters in the family of

God. We are equal in importance but not equal in function. That is why spiritual family comes before spiritual function. Equality in Christ lays the groundwork for the mutual respect of our individual strengths, insight, and perspectives. Peter's input was noteworthy.

Acts 15:10–12:

Now therefore why tempt ye God, to put a yoke upon the neck of the disciples, which neither our fathers nor we were able to bear?

But we believe that through the grace of the Lord Jesus Christ we shall be saved, even as they.

Then all the multitude kept silence, and gave audience to Barnabas and Paul, declaring what miracles and wonders God had wrought among the Gentiles by them.

Salvation is by grace, not by any work of our own. We believed in Jesus Christ and what he accomplished for us. As a result, we became part of the family of God along with Christian believers worldwide because we all share the same faith of Jesus Christ. When we believe and act on this truth, that is obedience to the household of faith spoken of in the Scriptures (Acts 6:7; Romans 1:5, 16:26).

Acts 15:22–23:

Then pleased it the apostles and elders with the whole church, to send chosen men of their own company to Antioch with Paul and Barnabas; *namely,* Judas surnamed Barsabas, and Silas, chief men among the brethren:

And they wrote *letters* by them after this manner; The apostles and elders and brethren *send* greeting unto the brethren which are of the Gentiles in Antioch and Syria and Cilicia.

They called the former Gentiles their "brethren" because they were now born again by the same heavenly Father. They knew that they were brothers and sisters through grace in the household of faith.

Acts 15:24:

Forasmuch as we have heard, that certain which went out from us have troubled you with words, subverting your souls, saying, *Ye must* be circumcised, and keep the law: to whom we gave no *such* commandment.

The apostles and elders, along with the whole church, agreed together and all gave approval to send letters (Acts 15:22 and 23). This is an example of Ephesians 4:3: "Endeavoring to keep the unity of the spirit in the bond of peace." Diligent effort was put forth to keep the spiritual unity God had made in His family.

Acts 15: The How of Subverting the Soul

Again, a deeper look into Acts 15:24 provides insight into how this "subverting your souls" took place. The subverting of their souls was like the believers were carried off as luggage and misplaced. This action violently turned them from what was right and unsettled them.[6] As a result, they were "troubled."

The word "troubled" in this verse is translated from the Greek word *tarassō*. Essentially, this Greek word means to *stir up, agitate, as water in a pool; of the mind, to stir up, trouble, disturb with various emotions; to render anxious or distressed.* Once people get agitated and their emotions begin to guide them, stress, anxiety, and fear soon follow. It is at that

---

6 ". . . to pack up baggage in order to take it to another place . . . turn away violently from a right state, to unsettle, subvert." (See endnotes under Joseph H. Thayer.)

point that any distortion or perversion of the truth can be introduced—even if it contradicts something people know to be true!

As a minister, I have cared for people when they were under deep emotional stress. In such situations, like when losing a loved one, people become very vulnerable. Simple decisions become difficult. Prior to this situation, they are moving confidently in life but then become unsure. "What am I going to do?" "How will I get through this?"

It is at these times of vulnerability, loving care and support is most needed. I have often advised people not to make life-changing decisions under these conditions. It is usually best to wait a period before such decisions are made. It was under similar emotional pressure that the believers in Acts 15 had their souls subverted.

We are not speaking here about being convinced by reason and evidence to the end somebody changes their mental posture or position on a subject. Not at all! What happened in Acts 15 was emotional bribery, manipulation, and seduction.

Such a stir of emotions can lead even knowledgeable Christians to entertain doubts about things they absolutely know to be true. Eventually, if exposed to enough of this malignant behavior and dialogue, people can refuse truth out of fear and intimidation, rather than as a result of knowledge and reason. Common sense departs; it is whisked away like a helium balloon from the grip of a small child who does not hold on to it. Astounding!

Galatians 1:6–7:

I [Paul] marvel that ye are so soon removed from him that called you into the grace of Christ unto another gospel: Which is not another; but there be some [that's people] that trouble [*tarassō*] you, and would pervert the gospel of [good news that pertains to] Christ.

Paul marveled that they were moved away from the grace that is in Christ Jesus to "another gospel." The word "another" in verse 6 means there are only two involved: 1) the true gospel, which is the good news of the grace of God in Christ Jesus, and 2) EVERYTHING ELSE.

So, how do believers get tricked into following something other than the truth? The answer is people. The "some" in verse 7 were people who agitated the Galatians' emotions. More than likely these people had access to the Galatians and were at the very least considered worth listening to if not even trusted. Often this deception and misdirection is done with words, accusations, threats, and intimidation against those who courageously speak the truth. Once emotions are agitated, then the perverting of the gospel has a forum. Lead with emotions, not reason, and manipulating others becomes a lot easier. This tactic is also highly successful in marketing in which an emotion is attached to a product or service. What is cleverly being "sold" is the emotion or feeling, not the product or service.

The word "pervert" here means to turn into something else, to change. When emotions rule and not the reason and the common-sense logic of the Word, perversions are introduced more easily. These errors are the opposite of the truth. This is what happened to the Apostle Paul. The Galatians knew the quality and fruit of the Word in his life, but someone orchestrated a cacophony of emotions among them that drowned out the truth. It was then easy to pervert the good news and turn the Galatians against the messenger. Suddenly Paul became their enemy.

Galatians 4:16–17:

Am I therefore become your enemy, because I tell you the truth?

They zealously affect you, but not well; yea, they would exclude you, that ye might affect them.

The Amplified Bible version of verse 17 is revealing: *These men [Judaizing teachers] are zealously trying to dazzle you [paying court to you, making much of you], but their purpose is not honorable or worthy or for any good. What they want to do is to isolate you [from us who oppose them], so that they may win you over to their side and get you to court their favor.*

These verses describe how people can be isolated and controlled by those to whom they look for help and guidance. This is how the Galatians were tricked into considering Paul was their enemy. A man who had told them the truth. As a result, they turned from him and embraced another gospel.

More than likely, there was a level of trust with those who were subverting their souls or the Galatians would not have even considered such assertions. Such deception begins with agitation, stirred up emotions through intimidation, and accusation. Then people become isolated and vulnerable to others' control. When some dare to speak up to expose how their leaders have departed from the truth, they often are labeled with terms that trigger more fear. They are identified as the enemy.

Spiritual unity *is not* maintained by excluding or eliminating people with whom we may disagree. Shutting down a healthy Word-centered dialogue is the tactic of those who fear the risk of being exposed.

The spiritual unity God intended is kept by the mutual determination of individuals who make the decision to act on truth in one accord. It takes an effort of humility, gentleness, and patience in love to invest time and heart to work with people. And when people value and live the truth above their own opinions and preferences, mutual respect in the household of faith keeps the unity and binds the faithful in peace.

Ephesians 4:1–3:

I therefore, the prisoner of the Lord, beseech you that ye walk worthy of the vocation wherewith ye are called,

With all lowliness and meekness, with longsuffering, forbearing one another in love;

Endeavouring to keep the unity of the Spirit in the bond of peace.

Spiritual unity begins with the "one calling" we all share. We all have received the same invitation from God to become His children. We strive for unity by living love that reflects His nature. It takes a lot of forgiveness. It is like the "one flesh" relationship in marriage. With a lot of love and a lot of forgiveness, that union between husband and wife develops. Likewise, we see the depth of forgiveness available when we think of how Jesus Christ forgave Judas, the very man who betrayed him. That's love!

The side we choose is God's side—He is always right. When Christians work against the unity of the spirit in the bond of peace, they faction off themselves into natural or *carnal* knowledge, and the grace of God is replaced by the works of men. Such was the Corinthian church.

I Corinthians 3:1–6:

And I, brethren, could not speak unto you as unto spiritual, but as unto carnal, *even* as unto babes in Christ.

I have fed you with milk, and not with meat: for hitherto ye were not able to *bear it*, neither yet now are ye able.

For ye are yet carnal [to be five-senses or natural-knowledge dominated, not Word-minded]: for whereas *there is* among you envying, and strife, and divisions, are ye not carnal, and walk as men?

For while one saith, I am of Paul; and another, I *am* of Apollos; are ye not carnal?

Who then is Paul, and who *is* Apollos, but ministers by whom ye believed, even as the Lord gave to every man?

I have planted, Apollos watered; but God gave the increase.

The Corinthians were not able to receive the teaching of spiritual matters—the deep things of God like spiritual unity. They saw life on the surface. They framed their lives inside of a carnal or natural-knowledge box. That is why they chose sides and preferred to talk about people, not the Word. How believers approach a problem or challenge determines, in large part, the outcome.

It has been a long-time and popular notion that during the Civil War, Abraham Lincoln was asked, "Whose side is God on?" His response was, "Sir, my concern is not whether God is on our side. My greatest concern is to be on God's side, for God is always right."

That is the position to anchor upon. It is not *who* is right but *what* is right. God and His Word are always right!

When we focus on who is right or on affiliations, that leads to focusing on people. The correct response is: "We stand with God and His Word."

Acts 15: The Results

We looked at Acts 15 and the Jerusalem council and that the apostles were present together in making an important decision. Let us look at the results.

Acts 16:4–5:

And as they went through the cities, they delivered them the decrees for to keep, that were ordained of the apostles and elders which were at Jerusalem.

And so were the churches established in the [household of] faith, and increased in number daily.

Look at the result—the churches (local Christian communities) were established and made stable in the household of faith. This indicates they acknowledged and believed that they were brothers and sisters through grace—the accomplished work of Christ. Each believer, whether previously Judean or Gentile, was an equal member of the family of God following the new birth. Each shared in the same salvation through the faith of Jesus Christ. Again, it is significant to note that the apostles (plural) were present to endorse this direction in Acts 15, which led to what unfolded in Acts 16.

Acts 21: What Is Right Versus Do What We Say

In contrast, let us now consider an event that took place in Acts 21. Several years later, after his conversion and dynamic missionary success, Paul headed to Jerusalem. However, the Scriptures clearly indicate that Paul really should *not* have gone to Jerusalem (Acts 20:22 and 23; 21:4, 10–12). God didn't want him to go. The household of believers told him not to go. Even a prophet came from Judea, where Jerusalem is located, and warned Paul not to go. But he went anyway.

The Apostle Paul's resistance to clear direction from God shows that even great leaders can have cloudy judgment if their personal desires are not balanced with God's wisdom and timing. Paul wrote the following in Romans.

Romans 10:1:

Brethren, my heart's desire and prayer to God for Israel is, that they might be saved.

God wanted even more than Paul for Israel to be saved. But free will is a boundary that God respects, and so people must be ready for salvation and want it. Salvation in Christ involves change. Israel had been under the Law for centuries, so change was not easy for most of them.

Also, timing may be a factor in such matters. God, who is all-knowing, knows the best timing. Perhaps Paul could have gone later, but the Word does not tell us. Paul was "bound in the spirit" (Acts 20:22), meaning he was not free to go, and he knew it. We need not be critical of Paul. Viewing this as a lesson provided for us is a good thing. To be successful, our desires should line up with God's wisdom, which includes His timing.

Now let us look at the response from some of the leaders and believers in Jerusalem who were present at that time.

Acts 21:18:

And the *day* following Paul went in with us [which would have included Luke] unto James; and all the elders were present.

Notice verse 18 does not mention the apostles, only James. James was a leader and was the Lord's half-brother (Mark 6:3). The elders were present with him, but where were the apostles? They were noticeably missing. How interesting! The Word does not tell us why, but we do know that they are not mentioned.

This notable absence in the Scriptures arrests our attention, especially because this is the same meeting location as in Acts 15—Jerusalem. It is in this context that the final occurrence of the word "disciple" appears in the Book of Acts (Acts 21:16) as if to underscore the futility of this remedial crusade.

This omission by God of the word "disciple" from this point forward is noteworthy and indicative of the bad fruit emanating from this

Jerusalem encounter. In other words, Paul's ministry was not received and, therefore, hindered to the end that no more mention is made of disciples converting and flourishing to spread the good news of the grace of God in Christ Jesus.

Acts 21:19:

And when he had saluted them, he declared particularly what things God had wrought among the Gentiles by his ministry.

Paul proclaimed the goodness of God and the deliverance He brought to those who believed the gospel. This is an example of how Christians today can praise their Heavenly Father and how He is working in their lives. When we are focused on God and His power, then it is relatively easy to discuss what is happening in our lives in terms of the wonderful things He is doing. Just like Paul, we are interested in declaring what God is doing in our lives. Let us look at the response.

Acts 21:20–22:

And when they heard it, they glorified the Lord, and said unto him, Thou seest, brother, how many thousands of Jews [Judeans, what was left of the once mighty Israel] there are which believe; and they are all zealous of the law:

And they are informed of thee, that thou teachest all the Jews [Judeans] which are among the Gentiles to forsake Moses, saying that they ought not to circumcise *their* children, neither to walk after the customs.

What is it therefore? the multitude must needs come together: for they will hear that thou art come.

Paul told them what God was doing. In response, they briefly acknowledged his words and then moved on to the matter they wanted to discuss. They wanted to inform Paul that his teachings were not *congruent* with the Law and what the Judeans had followed for centuries. Truthfully, Paul's teaching was not *contrary* to the Law. He taught that Christ was the fulfillment of the Law (Romans 10:4).

Paul taught the "next step" for God's people, as well as for all mankind, as God revealed it to him. He proclaimed an era of grace where the work of Jesus Christ is to be highlighted. Christ ushered in centuries of God's divine favor to man. No longer is man required to fulfill the works of the Law to be accepted and right before God. The Mosaic Law, in its scope and totality, was impossible to fulfill perfectly by anyone except Jesus Christ. God was ready to move ahead with man through grace.

God's grace gently moves man forward. Such a movement of God can be viewed as a building process or improvement, not necessarily a total replacement. God does not initiate anything haphazardly. He methodically introduces new periods or ages in His plan. These ages are differentiated simply by noting what God is offering to man and what He is requiring of man. Previous standards may not always be wholly discarded but improved upon as people move according to how God guides them at that time. Certain aspects of His plan, like circumcision, are over. They belong to the application of the past and may become figurative learning tools for us in the present.

Even things God initiates in our lives may have limits to their application, meaning that things may be right and useful for us for only a certain time. We are to "Prove all things; hold fast that which is good" (I Thessalonians 5:21). By way of His grace, God guides us beyond our self-prescribed comfort zones, even though we often insist, "It must be this way!" God's vision is greater than ours. What seems like greener pasture to us is not always the higher quality of life that God offers us daily. We need to be humble toward the change that God offers.

However, the Judeans in Acts 21 did not want to change and move on to where God was leading. Even though the Mosaic Law had ended with Jesus Christ, some Judeans wanted to remain under the yoke of the Old Testament Law.

Contrast Between Acts 15 and Acts 21

Acts 21:23:

Do therefore this that we say to thee . . .

There is quite a contrast between "Look what God has done" and "Do what we say." The leaders at Jerusalem gave Paul an assignment to engage in legalistic standards to endorse the Law. Paul states in Romans 10:4 that ". . . Christ is the end of the law . . . to every one that believeth." It is hard at times for man to accept that even things that God initiates, as great as they were for a time, like the Law, may have an end to them.

The Jerusalem leaders are an illustration of lording over God's people or top-down leadership. The knowledge of God's grace in Christ was knocking at their door via Paul's ministry and yet they moved to isolate Paul to control him. What did God want? Well, by this time Paul was ready to deliver the previously hidden truth regarding the revelation of the Body of Christ and the household of faith as much as he understood up to that point. He had already written I and II Thessalonians, Romans, I and II Corinthians, and Galatians. But the response from Jerusalem was, "Hey, praise God, that is great what you're doing Paul, but we want you to do what we say."

"Do what I say," as opposed to "Do what the Word says," exhibits a desire to control by those who lord over God's people. That is the contrast. A grace-era minister, following the day of Pentecost (Acts 2), only wants people to do what the Word says.

Let us note a key missing piece when Acts 15 is compared to Acts 21. The key missing piece is that the apostles are noticeably absent in Acts 21, and the results speak for themselves. In Acts 15 and 16, disciples were won to Christ when Paul was unrestricted to teach and preach. In Acts 21 and following, Paul was put in prison. And his ministry, in terms of unrestricted access, was at the very least hindered. It was not God's will that he was imprisoned.

When those whom God calls to minister are removed from the Christian ministry, we do not have the Christian ministry as God intended. Ministers are to fulfill their God-given purpose to care for the saints, which catalyzes the work of the ministry and the edifying of the Body of Christ.

Ephesians 4:8, 11–12:

Wherefore he saith, When he ascended up on high, he led captivity captive, and gave gifts [*domata*]⁷ unto men . . .

And he gave some, apostles; and some, prophets; and some, evangelists; and some, pastors and teachers [all of these are plural];

For the perfecting of the saints, for the work of the ministry, for the edifying of the body of Christ.

At its core, the Christian ministry is simple. It is about meeting the needs of people with love and the Word. It is not about positions or titles. Positions of service can provide access to a sphere of influence in

---

7   In Ephesians 4:8, the word "gifts" translated from the Greek plural noun *domata* emphasizes the gifts of service of verse 11 given for the common advantage in the church. See endnote for Joseph H. Thayer, *Thayer's Greek-English Lexicon of the New Testament*.

an organized manner to move the ministry forward. However, what is central to the Christian ministry is God's Word and the spiritual abilities God has given each of us to function together. These are the truths that need to be emphasized while making decisions and policies within the Christian ministry.

Simply, when people's needs are met, the work of the ministry moves forward, and the Word reaches those who are hungry for truth. Those who God calls to serve, working together, acknowledging the Word as the only real standard, is what provides for those needs to be met. Then the saints rise and contribute to the work of the ministry. Further, they develop their individual spiritual strengths as they freely take ownership of the gift of holy spirit, which builds the Body of Christ in love. Beautiful!

The word "perfecting" in verse 12 comes from the Greek word *katartismos*. It is the noun form of the Greek verb used for the action of mending fishing nets. Here it is used in the sense of making "fully ready… perfectly equipping…fully preparing" the saints to walk in newness of life (Romans 6:4). This is appropriate when we envision God's people gaining the full bounty of God's grace as they place their expectations in God and what He wrought in Christ (Ephesians 3:20).

We know that Christ within each of us needs no perfecting because the gift of holy spirit is already perfect (James 1:17) and created by God in righteousness and true holiness (Ephesians 4:24). However, each of us does need help in how we live it! Those called as gifts to the church are restorative agents as servants, helpers of the believers' joy, and free-will moral examples in word and deed. They help the believers grow and mature spiritually. These are the ministers of Romans 13. A true minister seeks the right connections with the Word that communicates to the individual for his or her personal walk with God.

Ephesians 4:13–16:

Till we all come in the unity of the faith [household faith], and of the knowledge of the Son of God, unto a perfect man, unto the measure of the stature of the fulness of Christ:

That we *henceforth* be no more children [infants], tossed to and fro, and carried about with every wind of doctrine, by the sleight of men, and cunning craftiness, whereby they lie in wait to deceive;

But speaking the truth in love, may grow up into him in all things, which is the head, *even* Christ:

From whom [Christ] the whole body fitly joined together and compacted by that which every joint supplieth, according to the effectual working in the measure of every part, maketh increase of the body unto the edifying of itself in love.

"Every joint supplieth according to the effectual working . . . of every part." This does not mean just one, two, three, or four people. It means everybody working together with great love, tenderness, and forgiveness. As "the perfecting of the saints" is accomplished and needs are met, people are inspired. Then, they utter those precious words, "What can I do to help?" Thankful believers simply want to serve. This is what leads to "the work of the ministry." Then edifying of the Body of Christ happens when spiritual strengths of service are contributed by all in love.

The Team Approach in the Christian Ministry

Whenever and wherever the Christian ministry is active, people serve at their best, and their individual qualities shine when they function as a team. Teams need leaders to catalyze needful change, lead the charge to advance amidst challenge, and champion unity. Whether they organically emerge or are already recognized as such, leaders play a vital role in the team environment in which everyone is encouraged to contribute and function.

Leaders do not necessarily need to have titles. Dads and moms lead, those with spiritual strengths in organization and administration lead, and any believer can lead as they contribute their unique spiritual strength in the Body of Christ in love.

The team approach, with obedience to the household of faith, is how the Body of Christ is to function. This is the best spiritual model for the Christian ministry. However, it is not easily carried out because self-serving agendas often creep in (Romans 16:17–18). The carnal "us and them" approach (I Corinthians 3:1–6) and our spiritual enemy (Ephesians 6:12) both disrupt spiritual unity. It is the unity of the spiritual Body under one head, Jesus Christ (Ephesians 4:15–16), where our unique spiritual strengths complement one another—just like parts of the human body work together harmoniously.

I Corinthians 12:27–28:

Now ye are the body of Christ, and members in particular.

And God hath set some in the church, first apostles, secondarily prophets, thirdly teachers, after that miracles, then gifts of healings, helps [in the category of support], governments [in the category of organization], diversities of tongues.

These verses in the twelfth chapter of I Corinthians are in the context of spiritual matters and are certainly "meat," not "milk." These verses are for those who are mature or desire to become mature. Those who are mature in Christ recognize the importance of the interdependent and spiritual functions of the members in the Body.

Represented here are the ministers called as gifts to the church, the energized manifestation of the spirit, and other ministries that support and organize. These can all work together in unity as a team. Therefore, it is spiritual functioning that we should acknowledge in a team context, not solely focus on titles and positions.

What Can We Do?

When the ministers called of God are taken out of the picture, as we saw in the comparison of Acts 15 and 21, people tend toward legalism and centralization of authority. Then, we no longer have the biblical approach to the Christian ministry that God intends. Having checks and balances in authority is wise. People with authority can get deceived and, if left unchecked, often are.

The Founding Fathers of the United States understood this. They divided the power or authority of the government into three separate parts to check and balance each other. It is enshrined in the Constitution of the United States and it allows a nation of free people to co-exist despite our many differences.

In the spiritual realm, God's Word is our standard.

Matthew 4:4:

But he answered and said, It is written, Man shall not live by bread alone, but by every word that proceedeth out of the mouth of God.

Jesus Christ, representing all that is good in life, spoke directly to the Devil, representing all that is evil in life. He said, "It is written," which is the right response in all life's situations.

We began this chapter by noting that when believers reach an impasse among themselves, they should not ask *who* is right, but *what* is right. The correct response is, "God and His Word are right." When we stand with God on His Word, everything else sorts itself out. The impasse becomes less difficult to traverse because we know the truth.

If we find ourselves in a situation where spiritual authority in the Christian ministry seems to be lording over God's people, here are some practical things we can do:

- Speak up when appropriate and address the issue. You can meet in person or call or write. But be truly kind, loving, clear, and firm. As we love, God is at work within us.
- Review I Corinthians 13 on the love of God. We do not want to harbor ill will toward anyone. We harbor no bitterness, no anger, just the love of God for people. The love of God does not fail.
- Require a biblical answer to your questions to the end you are satisfied. "It is Written" is how Jesus Christ handled challenges. This approach gives glory to God. Requesting "chapter and verse" for what people say is an honest and objective biblical approach.
- Prove the Word to yourself. Romans 12:2 says ". . . prove what is that good, and acceptable, and perfect, will of God." Acts 17:11 talks about the Bereans who ". . . were more noble than those in Thessalonica, in that they received the word with all readiness of mind, and searched the scriptures daily, whether those things were so." They were checking to see if those things being spoken and taught were right. That is making the Word your own.
- Pray abundantly and open your heart to God. He listens, and He answers.

When the leaders at Jerusalem rejected Paul's message of grace in Christ but instead returned back to the legalistic standards of the Mosaic Law, they failed. They failed because they rejected what God was in the moment moving among men. The Christian leadership dilemma is most vividly revealed at critical and significant junctures in life. It is exposed by the choices each person makes. We can either choose God's path or the path of men. God's paths do not always conflict with man, but when they do, the choice for the Christian leader is simple. Choose God, for He is always right.

It can be difficult to move beyond what one is accustomed to. We have all perhaps experienced this at one time or another. What helps us move on is trusting in God (Proverbs 3:5 and 6) to guide us along the path where He is currently moving at the time. Moving ahead with grace and keeping the faith is something Paul did. We can too.

The next chapter goes into more detail on recognizing a movement of God.

Chapter 3

ONE ACCORD—*HOMOTHUMADON*

Now we are going to consider the Greek word *homothumadon* to gain a deeper understanding of God's heart and wisdom. When studied in the Book of Acts, this Greek word pinpoints a unique characteristic of believers in the first century and how they moved with God while functioning together. It can certainly help us to move ahead with grace in our endeavors.

"Homothumadon" Defined

In its basic form, this word means "with one accord," as it is translated in the King James Bible. Specifically, it means "with one mind, unanimously." Rarely in life do we see such a high level of agreement among men because usually, men do not consider God's heart and wisdom. Reaching this *one mind* condition is not accomplished by natural knowledge or five-senses reasoning among men, but rather it is by purposely seeking God who is able to aide and guide. Therefore Word-centered prayer is especially important. As believers, our success in reaching *one accord* is measured by our willingness to get God involved. It can only be accomplished *with* God.

Looking into this word deeper reveals more of the mindset of these pioneers of Christianity. These believers were all of one accord, with one mind, unanimous in their purpose and involvement. One reference describes it as:

> "A unique Greek word . . . [that] helps us understand the uniqueness of the Christian community. *Homothumadon* is a compound of two words meaning 'to rush along' and 'in unison.' The image is almost musical; a number of notes are sounded which, while different, harmonise in pitch and tone. As the instruments of a great concert under the direction of a concert master, so the Holy Spirit blends together the lives of members of Christ's church."

This word expresses an exceptional characteristic of the early Christian community which arrests our attention. Exploring it further reveals the two Greek words that make up this compound word are: *homos*, which in Greek means "same," and *thumos*, which in Greek means "passion." Further, one scholar characterizes *thumos* as "an intense passion of the mind." So, *homothumadon* is a symphony of souls that surpasses more than a mental agreement. When used of the things of God, there is an individual passion for a movement of God.

Such unified passion could be likened to a sports team locked into one purpose to win the big game—everyone on that team is completely invested with heart, soul, mind, and strength. The members of the team are of one passion to win that game. This is like the concept of *homothumadon*.

There are seven positive occurrences of *homothumadon* in the Book of Acts, and one in Romans, that demonstrate how believers obtained godly results from their efforts. In contrast, there are four worldly occurrences (Acts 7:57, 12:20, 18:12, and 19:29) that clearly show men working to fulfill their own agenda and are adversarial to the true God. These occurrences refer to politically engineered agreements to gain an advantage over others. These four occurrences reveal the parasitical, leeching nature of Satan.

Knowing our true enemy in life helps to frame our struggles to our advantage. Our efforts are not wasted on symptoms, but we get to the real cause of the spiritual struggles we face. Our true enemy, and the cause of so many of man's ills is Satan.

The name Satan, from the Hebrew language and later adopted into Greek, means "opponent" or "adversary" and carries with it the connotation "to attack, (fig.) accuse." Satan is the spiritual adversary of God, Christ, and God's people. He endeavors to deceive, manipulate, and eventually enslave people to carry out his purposes, which are to steal, kill, and destroy (John 10:10). We will see Satan's insidious and adversarial activity against Godly inspired unity is revealed as we consider the occurrences of *homothumadon*.

In the context of each of the seven positive occurrences in the Book of Acts, there is a movement of God that results in unity of purpose and like-minded action by believers. These movements involve setting the practical foundation for the church or are in response to a conflict that arises from without or within the Christian church. In each of these examples, a profitable solution emerges and is expressed in a *homothumadon* unity of the believers.

The leaders involved played a key role in each situation. It was with humility followed by their energy of conviction that each leader recognized God at work. Then leaders inspired and guided followers as a team. Each member of the team humbly added their own personal energy of conviction, enthusiasm, and commitment to what God was moving. That was what built a genuine *homothumadon*, a state of "one accord."

First Positive Occurrence

Acts 1:14:

These all continued with one accord [*homothumadon*] in prayer and supplication, with the women, and Mary the mother of Jesus, and with his brethren.

"These" refers to the 11 apostles of verse 13. By this time Judas had departed. It was after the ascension of Jesus Christ (Acts 1) and before the day of Pentecost (Acts 2). The "one accord" is with one mind or unanimously.

In this first occurrence, the apostles led the way in carrying out Jesus Christ's teachings and instruction. The followers included Mary, the mother of Jesus, and Jesus's brethren (Matthew 13:55 and 56). Jesus Christ was no longer present on earth, but he left specific instructions for them to abide in Jerusalem until they would be endued with power from on high (Luke 24:49). A great key in transitional times, such as Jesus's departure and the apostles starting to lead, is the concept of *homothumadon*. They did not know the fullness of what would happen or exactly when it would happen, but this did not stop them from remaining unified and moving ahead on what they did know to do while trusting God to fill in the missing pieces

None of us know the future, so we are all familiar to some degree with what these believers would have experienced. Yet, they moved ahead with what they *did* know. In transition, they stayed focused on what does not change, God (*For I am the LORD, I change not* . . . Malachi 3:6). How revealing a lesson this is in times of transition. Our circumstances may change, but God does not. He is a steady rock beneath us and always faithful.

In hindsight, we have the benefit of reading the Scriptures that tell us of the gift of holy spirit and the "all truth" (John 16:13) that Jesus told his followers would be offered. This "all truth" includes the seven church epistles, which detail the knowledge of the accomplished work of Christ. The gospels of Matthew, Mark, Luke, and John *chronicle* the work of Christ while on earth. These letters from the Apostle Paul, Romans through Thessalonians, take a deep dive into and *explain* the work of Christ and its relevance to the Christian. Acts is the practical transition between the four gospels and the church epistles.

For the believers, not having this scriptural documentation of what they were about to receive did not stop them from acting on what they knew. They relied on and trusted in God and what Jesus had taught them. In the transitions of life, we may not have all the details. We may know only a general direction in which God wants us to move. As we move in this direction, God fills in the details as we act (hence the Book of Acts!). Remembering He is trustworthy and faithful is essential to success.

Acts is such an appropriate name for this transitional revelation between the ministry of Jesus Christ and the unveiling of the complete Christian doctrine as noted in the epistles of Paul. The Books of Acts shows believers learning to embrace and take ownership and use the gift of holy spirit, even when not all the details of the gift were revealed and understood. We may not know all the details of what God has prepared either, but that should not stop us from moving ahead.

Second Positive Occurrence

Acts 2:1:

And when the day of Pentecost was fully come, they were all with one accord [*homothumadon*] in one place.

What God did on the day of Pentecost was the fulfillment of His plan to redeem mankind through the promised seed of the woman, as first noted in Genesis 3:15. God moved to aid and restore man to his original harmony and unity in God's presence. This was done on the heels of man's disobedience to God when sin and death were allowed to enter the world. God's plan to restore man to a right state with Him reached its fruition here as recorded in Acts 2:1. God was preparing the answer to man's challenges and ills long before time began.

II Timothy 1:9:

Who hath saved us, and called *us* with an holy calling, not according to our works, but according to his own purpose and grace, which was given us in Christ Jesus before the world began.

The phrase "before the world began" can be translated "before the times of the ages."[8] Before the wheels of time in God's universal clock began to turn, God had foreknowledge of our rescue through Christ. This seems incomprehensible. For perspective, this indicates that before God created the heavens and the earth as recorded in Genesis 1:1, He had already set our purpose and grace in Christ. When "the beginning" was we do not know. There is plenty of physical evidence that eons of

---

8   The existence, arrangement, and movement of matter in varying degrees of concentration or in expansive relation (from molecular to celestial) is directly related to the concept and measurement of time.

time have passed since then. But what we do know is that the ages of time, as best we understand, as a measurement, had a beginning. The inception of matter coincides with the inception of time. This all began with the act of God recorded in Genesis 1:1 (for further references to the correlation of matter and time please see also Genesis 1:14–19; Joshua 10:12–14).

Isaiah 46:10:

Declaring the end from the beginning, and from ancient times *the things* that are not *yet* done, saying, My counsel shall stand, and I will do all my pleasure.

Romans 8:28–31:

And we know that all things work together for good to them that love God, to them who are the called according to *his* purpose.

For whom he did foreknow [the Greek word *proginōskō* to know beforehand][9], he also did predestinate [the Greek word *proorizō* determine beforehand][10], *to be* conformed to the image of his Son, that he might be the firstborn among many brethren.

---

9   The word *proginōskō* implies an experiential, observable, and therefore verifiable knowledge. When speaking about such foreknowledge it can be applied to man if a person has experienced, observed, and therefore can verify something that occurred in the past. When speaking about such foreknowledge in the future, meaning to experience, observe, and therefore verify something before it happens, this can only be applied to God and where and when He may reveal such knowledge to man. See endnote for Gerhard Kittel.

10   The word *proorizō* does not involve God orchestrating our freewill decisions on earth as if our destiny is already set but rather based on *proginōskō* implying God's experiential, observable, and therefore verifiable knowledge of our decisions ahead of time, God determines His responses to our decisions. See endnote for Finis, Jennings Drake, page 292.

Moreover whom he did predestinate [*proorizō*] them he also called: and whom he called, them he also justified: and whom he justified, them he also glorified.

What shall we then say to these things? If God *be* for us, *who can be* against us?

So, the giving of holy spirit on the day of Pentecost shows the first human beings who received the initial outpouring of what God had prepared for us long ago. God knew us ahead of time. When we as believers are genuinely in "one accord," we are in the best position to enjoy the amazing things God has prepared for us like our calling, our justification, and our glory.

Acts 2:2–4:

And suddenly there came a sound from heaven as of a rushing mighty wind, and it filled all the house where they were sitting.

And there appeared unto them cloven tongues like as of fire, and it sat upon each of them.

And they were all filled with the Holy Ghost, and began to speak with other tongues, as the Spirit gave them utterance.

This second occurrence of *homothumadon* documents that there were twelve apostles. This included Matthias, who was added to the original eleven (Acts 1:26). The twelve were in one accord; they were with one passion in the temple, and they took ownership of the gift of holy spirit and used the power from on high by speaking in tongues. The giving of the gift of holy spirit is a clear movement of God as opposed to something initiated by men. They followed the instruction that Jesus Christ personally gave them on the day of his ascension.

Acts 1:8:

But ye shall receive [the Greek word *lambano*—meaning to take ownership in order to use[11]] power, after that the Holy Ghost is come upon you: and ye shall be witnesses unto me both in Jerusalem, and in all Judaea, and in Samaria, and unto the uttermost part of the earth.

Taking ownership of and using the gift of holy spirit is clearly God's heart and wisdom for the church. The power Jesus Christ spoke to his followers about was displayed on the day of the feast of Pentecost. Following the twelve speaking in tongues, Peter and the other apostles taught the crowd of "devout men out of every nation" (Acts 2:5) about Jesus Christ. These devout followers of Judaism had come to Jerusalem to celebrate this feast. When their hearts were stirred by the words regarding Christ, they realized that God had "made that same Jesus, whom ye crucified, both Lord and Christ." So, they asked, "What shall we do?" and Peter responded.

---

11   The understanding of the Greek word *lambano* indicates ownership and active utilization as the following reveals, "to take with the hand, lay hold of, *any pers. or thing in order to use it . . .* to take what is one's own, to take to one's self, to make one's own," Joseph H. Thayer, *Thayer's Greek-English Lexicon of the New Testament.* "There is a certain distinction between *lambano* and *dechomai* (more pronounced in the earlier, classical use), in that in many instances *lambano* suggests a self-prompted taking, whereas *dechomai* more frequently indicates a welcoming or an appropriating reception" (Grimm-Thayer), see W.E. Vine, Merrill F. Unger, William White, Jr., *Vine's Complete Expository Dictionary of Old and New Testament Words.* "The original etymological meaning—Acc. to Schmidt, 210 f. this is still predominant in class. usage, is to 'grasp,' 'to seize.' It develops in two directions. The first is active, 'to take,' 'to bring under one's control on one's own initiative." See endnote for Gerhard Kittel, *Theological Dictionary of the New Testament,* Vol. 4.

Acts 2:37–38:

Now when they heard *this*, they were pricked in their heart, and said unto Peter and to the rest of the apostles, Men *and* brethren, what shall we do?

Then Peter said unto them, Repent, and be baptized every one of you in the name of Jesus Christ for the remission of sins, and ye shall receive [*lambanō*—take ownership to use] the gift of the Holy Ghost [holy spirit].

This same pattern continued with Peter when he reached out to the Gentiles[12] and then later when Paul guided and encouraged people to take ownership and use the gift of holy spirit (Acts 10:45 and 46; 19:2 and 6; I Corinthians 14:5 and 39).

Notice that the apostles were first to take ownership of and use the gift of holy spirit—power from on high. The growth and development of the first-century church was advanced by the leaders who were servants, helpers of the believers' joy, and examples. Leaders—those who take the initiative to move with God whether recognized as leaders or not or having titles or not—set the spiritual pace and example as catalysts among people to reach *homothumadon*. Such leaders are moral agents for Christ-like transformation from the heart that begins with themselves and then spreads to others. Peter and the apostles clearly evidenced the right type of leadership.

It is important to understand, however, that a genuine *homothumadon* is not obtained by merely joining a group or going along with the crowd. It's about personal conviction on the truth regarding what God is moving in Christ at any given place and time. Such a movement is

---

12 ". . . a number of people living together bound together by like habits and customs [in the plural] . . . In the O.T. those who are not of Israel, and in the N.T. those who are neither of Israel nor of the Church . . ." See endnote for Ethelbert W. Bullinger, pp. 316–317.

not static. Rather, it is dynamic and inspired by God Himself. Often God's unmistakable timing helps us recognize when He is moving. This wonder can only be achieved with God's involvement. The signature of God is perfect timing. That is one way we know He is moving in a situation.

The apostles and the early church believers did not know the fullness of what they had received because the seven church epistles had yet not been written. The Mystery of the one Body of Christ had not been revealed at this point. But this did not stop them from moving with God as He continued to aid and guide them. Believers move with God as He leads and guides them.

Third Positive Occurrence

This movement of God, as characterized by unanimous passion among the brethren, moved from the group of apostles to the fellowship of believers (Acts 2:37–38). The third occurrence of *homothumadon* came after the apostles led people into receiving the gift of holy spirit. Peter and the other apostles taught the Word regarding Jesus Christ, and the people were inspired to act. But they needed direction on what to do. Peter guided the people into using the gift of holy spirit by speaking in tongues.[13] This is a practical cornerstone of the Christian experience—take ownership and use the gift of holy spirit. What follows is a developing community of believers later called Christians.

The third occurrence in Acts 2:46 follows Peter and the eleven standing up to hold forth the Word and the acceptance by the people to take as their own God's most precious gift. They were truly spiritual pioneers on the grace frontier.

---

13 God is offering His gift by way of the faith of Jesus Christ to countless souls across the world (Acts 17:31). Taking this very special gift as one's own and using it is a gesture of love back to the one who gave it.

Acts 2:46–47:

And they, continuing daily with one accord [*homothumadon*] in the temple, and breaking bread from house to house, did eat their meat with gladness and singleness of heart.

Praising God, and having [holding[14]] favour [grace] with [with a view to] all the people. And the Lord added to the church daily such as should be saved.

They continued daily with one accord—with one passion! Everyone with their own enthusiasm and commitment changed their lifestyle to reflect having received the gift of holy spirit by grace and not of their own works (Ephesians 2:8). This was revolutionary to those who were steeped in the works of the Mosaic Law for *centuries*. They each held on to this grace and held it out to others for their benefit. What a community!

They continued daily in unison in the temple. They also went to each other's houses and enjoyed meals together, and they had joy in their hearts.

This "continuing daily" is interesting because this lifestyle change came from their hearts. It was not superficial. They pursued fellowship one with another based on what they had been taught. True Christian fellowship is a mutual invitation and acceptance to share in the accomplished work of Christ that produces praise to God. We can do the same today.

These bloodline Israelites, Judeans, and converts to Judaism embraced salvation and the gift of holy spirit through grace. Their lives had been saturated with the Law. They were preoccupied with their own

---

14 ". . . to have and hold, implying present, continued having, lasting possession," See endnotes for Ethelbert W. Bullinger, *A Critical Lexicon and Concordance to the English and Greek New Testament*, p. 354.

works. Now they were entering a life of grace by the accomplished work of another, Jesus Christ.

Acts 2:42–43:

And they continued stedfastly in the apostles' doctrine and fellowship, and in breaking of bread, and in prayers.

And fear [respect] came upon every soul: and many wonders and signs were done by the apostles.

They shared grace which involved the Word (the apostle's doctrine) among themselves and by breaking of bread and prayers. The fellowship was the sharing of what they had just discovered that each had in common—the accomplished work of Christ. It was not their background or lineage, as one might suppose, but rather what God had offered to them through Christ. This is what dynamically changed and unified each of them. This is what God was moving in the church. These first-century believers freely joined themselves to each other in a community of the followers of the Lord Jesus Christ. The transformation was one soul at a time. As a result, a deep respect developed one for another. The mutual grace, God's unmerited divine favor through Christ, impacted them that much. Mutual respect, because of the common faith shared by all, is the first practical step to obedience to the household of faith (Acts 6:7; Romans 1:5, 16:26).

Personal Conviction

Each individual believer is to build this one accord, one passion, with God and not just simply agree with people. Personal ambition should not be mistaken for personal conviction. Those who have only personal ambition often compromise on what they know to be right to justify their aspirations. Personal conviction is a resolute mindset someone has when they stick to what they believe is right regardless of what others think and say or the obstacles they face. This does not mean that those who have personal conviction cannot change their mind. They can. However, they do it because they believe it is right, not because they fall prey to the pressure from others.

Personal conviction, beginning with leaders, is essential. The Christian leadership dilemma is fueled by leaders that lack moral fiber and the personal conviction to say and do what is right. Consequently, those that follow their example lose their footing and stability much like someone swimming at the beach can easily be carried out to sea by a rip current. Without personal conviction someone is not really a part of a *homothumadon*, as the Word notes. The whole process begins with God. Then good leaders—those who take the initiative to move with God— become convinced. And then others follow God's guiding hand. As God moves, these leaders are those who recognize and move, setting the pace and right moral example for the rest to follow.

II Timothy 2:1, 6–7:

Thou therefore, my son, be strong in the grace that is in Christ Jesus.

The husbandman that laboureth must be first partaker of the fruits.

Consider what I say; and the Lord give thee understanding in all things.

Timothy, as a leader, was encouraged to be strong in the grace that is in Christ Jesus. Leaders cannot lead others to a lifestyle of grace if they do not live it first. The "husbandman" here is a word for a farmer who labors. God put nature all around us, illustrating the principle of cause and effect. It is so visible, especially to farmers. Because seasonally they see the seed planted, growing, and then harvested. Anyone who has ever farmed knows that farming takes *labor*. It is not a job for a lazy person.

Similarly, the Word is not truly built in someone's life without *effort*. This labor is not necessarily measured in time (e.g., studying ten hours a day) but in heart and focus. Laboring in the Scriptures is not exclusively an academic or a scholarly activity. It is a deliberate, heartfelt endeavor. This labor has more to do with motive and humility than what many people might realize.

We each have strengths to contribute to the fellowship of believers, but we are not all biblical scholars. We do not need to be. The apostles were noted by skeptics of the time as "unlearned and ignorant men" or "illiterate persons, untrained in the schools," and "uneducated, common men" (Acts 4:13). By their critics' standards, they were not even *capable* of having an advanced spiritual education. Regardless, they did advance, thanks to their humble and resolute hearts to seek God. They replaced worldly thoughts and practices with godly ones that Jesus had taught them. This is the labor we must engage in. Draining the pool of stagnant and contaminated mental practices of this world makes room for the fresh, clean, and spiritually satisfying water of life.

Planting the Word in our hearts—listening to it, reading it, studying it, and considering it deeply—brings us to the point where we are convinced of the truth, and we act on it in love. Without personal conviction, people often look to others to make decisions for them. Personal conviction is aided by honest reflection and undistracted thought time. Removing, or at least reducing, distractions is a key component to honest reflection. The heart of the believer yearns for God and deeply considers His Word to shed light on the path that leads to Him.

The words "must be" in II Timothy 2:6 mean "it is necessary." It is necessary to be first partaker of the fruits. A believer who genuinely sows the Word in his heart will see the positive results. God assures us that we will see good fruit, or benefits, when we sow the Word. God never uses anybody. He wants each believer to benefit first from doing His

Word. When we see the fruit of God's Word for ourselves, our personal conviction deepens. Then we can help others. The salvation wholeness and fruit of a leader's life is what truly impacts the lives of others (I Timothy 4:16).

"Consider" in II Timothy 2:7 is directed to one person, Timothy. This word is translated from a Greek verb *noeō*. In this verse, its Greek grammatical construction makes it a command to be maintained continually. This means that the challenge set before Timothy is to keep sowing the Word in his heart, to keep on considering it.

This word "consider" is written in the singular form. The individual, Timothy, needed to decide for himself to be strong in God's grace and labor in the Word. When we apply this verse to our own lives, we see that each of us individually must decide to consider the Word. It says ". . . the Lord give thee," which makes the same point because in this verse "thee" is a singular pronoun. This is not an invitation for "group thinking" or "deciding by committee." This individual responsibility to consider describes the basis of a *homothumadon* action.

"Understanding" in the same verse is from the Greek noun *sunesis*, which comes from the verb *suniēmi*, meaning "to bring together . . . to come together." This word *sunesis* reflects a "union" in its meaning and can be illustrated by a flowing together "of two rivers" into one.

I have stood on the banks of the confluence of two rivers coming together to form one. The combined flow of water is awesome, and from that point forward the river is a much more dynamic, versatile, and powerful force. Our hearts and lives can be like that when we understand the things of God. A great place to begin this understanding is to recognize the simplicity of the lessons of nature, like the effect of two rivers flowing together causing a greater flow. Like the rivers, we combine or add to what we already know and keep learning about God. He is inexhaustible. As we stay receptive and humble our "river of understanding" regarding God will continue to increase.

As we continue to sow the Word in our hearts and apply it in our lives with a forward-looking heart, things begin to make sense. The truth brings spiritual understanding as the concepts flow together, especially when we apply them. So much understanding, the flowing together, happens when we act on the Word and do it. This spiritual understanding can grow through an entire lifetime.

Fourth Positive Occurrence

In the context of each of these first three occurrences of *homothumadon* in the Book of Acts, there is a movement of God that sets a foundation upon which believers can live, grow, and develop. In Acts 4 is the fourth occurrence. This is yet another movement of God, but here it concerns a conflict that arises from outside of the church. The church was attacked, and the believers went to God with one voice because only with Him could they determine how best to respond in true *homothumadon* fashion.

This fourth occurrence took place after religious leaders of the day attacked the movement of God's Word, specifically targeting Peter and John with threats. As is often the case, going unnoticed was Satan in the background fomenting the attack.

Peter and John were involved in the healing of a man who had been lame from birth. This miraculous healing brought many in the community to side with Peter and John. And it placed public pressure on the religious authorities to release Peter and John after holding them overnight to somehow punish them for teaching the people about Jesus Christ. Once released, they went back to their own company and reported all that the chief priests and elders said unto them. And then in verse 24 came the believers' response.

Acts 4:24:

And when they heard that, they lifted up their voice to God with one accord [*homothumadon*]; and said, Lord, thou *art* God, which hast made heaven, and earth, and the sea, and all that in them is:

They recognized God as the maker of all things and the source of all life. This includes the principle of cause and effect so abundantly on display in this beautiful world we live in. God's sovereign majesty as the originator of all matter and living things sets the foundation for this prayer.

This recorded prayer (verses 24–30) does not indicate they said these words in unison as if a script were handed out. The emphasis is on unity in the content of the prayer. Likely, as one person prayed, they all believed together. However, the way this prayer was orchestrated we do not know. What we do know is that it was expressed in one "voice" [singular], with "one accord" [*homothumadon*]. *Homothumadon* emanates from the heart and runs much deeper than simply speaking in unison, like a chant. Unless every heart is all in, there is no *homothumadon*.

Acts 4:29:

And now, Lord, behold their threatenings: and grant unto thy servants, that with all boldness they may speak thy word.

They were unified to speak God's Word with boldness in response to the conflict coming from without the church. God moved and worked in them, and they responded by speaking the Word with boldness. The boldness mentioned here began within the church by leaders who clearly saw the power and majesty of the Lord their God. This boldness registered with the religious leaders who opposed them (Acts 4:13).

Acts 4:30–31:

By stretching forth thine hand to heal; and that signs and wonders may be done by the name of thy holy child [servant] Jesus.

And when they had prayed, the place was shaken where they were assembled together; and they were all filled with the Holy Ghost, and they spake the word of God with boldness.

That is the action that they took as God was moving, inspiring, and working with them. This prayer to speak the Word boldly followed by healing, signs, and wonders demonstrates what a movement of God looks like in response to persecution. In the face of intimidation, God does not expect His people to back down or cower in fear, because He does not. He moves within His people to be fearless in declaring His Word of deliverance—even when the opposition endeavors to bully them into submission.

Grace and Giving

Acts 4:32–33:

And the multitude of them that believed were of one heart and of one soul: neither said any *of them* that ought of the things which he possessed was his own; but they had all things common.

And with great power gave the apostles witness of the resurrection of the Lord Jesus: and great grace was upon them all.

Giving out of what God already has given us is an immutable principal when it comes to giving to others. We can see this in action as a result of the "great grace" among the believers. Grace affected how they looked at each other and physical/material things. The phrase "neither said any of them that ought of the things which he possessed was his own" does not mean they had no personal or private property. Rather, it reflects a generous attitude of wanting to give from what God already had given them to meet needs.

The deeper truth behind this comes from understanding that "The earth is the Lord's and the fullness thereof" (Psalm 24:1; I Chronicles 29:10–16). We are stewards of the physical and material things in life for a time while we are on earth. Because we brought nothing physical or material into this life, we certainly will leave this life the same way; it all stays here (I Timothy 6:7).

The word "common" in verse 32 means it was not considered sacred, in the sense of bound or forbidden. It is the opposite of something having restricted access and, therefore, is exclusive and cannot be touched. Their personal property was not sacred to them. The word "common" reflects an attitude toward physical/material property and is not a declaration that everything is communal or owned by everyone. Therefore, the phrase "all things common" does not contradict the idea that people can own things and steward them and do what they determine with those things. The point here in Acts is that each responded in their heart along this line, "What I own is not off limits—mine, mine, mine—if it meets a need."

This idea is reiterated in the next chapter when a couple who owned and sold "a possession" was told by Peter that, "Whiles it remained [the land], was it not thine own? And after it was sold, was it not in thine own power?" (Acts 5:4) Relinquishing ownership of private property is not what these verses in Chapter 4 are about, but they are about having an attitude that all physical and material things come from God, and the use of them does not need to be restricted. Appropriately sharing, as each of us decides in our own heart, can bring great joy to our lives, and frees us from the tyranny of physical possessions. Sharing is liberating and a lot more joyful.

We see that "great grace was upon them all." Such grace among the believers affected how they looked at each other, and the physical/material things they owned. There was a need among their brethren who stayed in Jerusalem after the feast of Pentecost, which was a one-day celebration (Acts 2). These devout followers got born again, and because they had not planned to stay long after the celebration, they obviously needed food and shelter. By the grace of God, the community of believers helped each other. It was grace that filled their hearts and fueled their giving. They understood that all things belong to God and as stewards they were willing to share. It was God's favor, His grace from heaven to man on earth, that was on display.

Acts 4:34–35:

Neither was there any among them that lacked: for as many as were possessors of lands or houses sold them, and brought the prices of the things that were sold,

And laid *them* down at the apostles' feet: and distribution was made unto every man according as he had need.

The phrase "Neither was there any among them that lacked" refers to no one being "needy." Having need and being "needy" are two different things. When the Apostle Paul wrote in Philippians 4:11, "Not that I speak in respect of want . . .", he indicated that his conversation was not dominated by his personal needs. His conversation was dominated by describing the God who supplied his need (Philippians 4:19). There is nothing wrong with making a need known, but it is not something to talk about all the time. Such conversation can reflect a "needy" attitude, and this is not how these early Christians were characterized.

There are three actions that the first-century church did that are expressed in Greek verbs noted in verse 35. More than one believer sold lands and houses and "brought the prices of the things that were sold" and "laid *them* down." This laying down is the first action expressed in a plural verb, meaning there was more than one person who did this. Next, "distribution was made" is a singular verb, meaning the distribution was one at a time. Then finally the distribution was as ". . . he [meaning any] had [singular verb] need [singular]." So, these three actions—*plural* laying down, *singular* distribution, and *singular* need, paint a clear picture of how the early Christians extended grace to one another in terms of material things.

What these three verbs describe is a perfect balance of supply and demand. The laying down was done by more than one person, the distribution was done singularly, meaning one at a time, as any had need. This means that when a singular need came up, the supply was there to cover it. The giving was plural, the need was singular, and the distribution was singular. This is one of the great examples of grace, partnering with God, giving to others who had a need. And it is a result of prayer and boldness in a *homothumadon* manner.

All giving begins with God. He is the source. God provides for us His plenty, which is always more than enough. Thanksgiving to God is the recognition that He is the source of supply in our lives. And we steward in this life what He supplies. Grace embodies both thankful recognition to God and giving in love to others.

This retaining grace as our own to share with others is how the early church operated. Understanding grace in this light is what is meant by being a "cheerful giver" in II Corinthians 9:7. This understanding in the heart of the child of God provides, like nothing else, a sense of freedom regarding physical and material things.

Fifth Positive Occurrence

Following the great prayer and deliverance of Acts 4, many were inspired to help their fellow brothers and sisters who had need. This specifically was because many who had come to Jerusalem for the feast of Pentecost remained and had need. The believers exhibited a great heart of giving to help one another.

Now the fifth occurrence of *homothumadon* follows in Acts 5. This occurrence is in the context of a practical conflict from within the church. It deals with a couple who endeavored to infiltrate this young Christian community with deception. Their names were Ananias and Sapphira, and they conducted themselves deceitfully regarding money. This error was "of the heart" with the intent to deceive. Such attitudes were not consistent with the one accord in the fellowship seen up to this point.

The key to understanding what happened is in verses 1–4.

Acts 5:1–4:

But a certain man named Ananias, with Sapphira his wife, sold a possession,

And kept back *part* of the price, his wife also being privy *to it*, and brought a certain part, and laid *it* at the apostles' feet.

But Peter said, Ananias, why hath Satan filled thine heart to lie to the Holy Ghost [God], and to keep back *part* of the price of the land?

Whiles it remained, was it not thine own? and after it was sold, was it not in thine own power? why hast thou conceived this thing in thine heart? thou hast not lied unto men, but unto God.

As expectations in God rise, the Word of God gains momentum and believers speak the Word boldly, and signs and wonders are done in the name of Jesus Christ. The spiritual light penetrates any darkness and becomes brighter and brighter in and around the fellowship of believers. Others outside the Christian community are attracted to the truth but not always for the right reasons. When the light of God's Word is bright enough, the darkness becomes exposed. When Ananias and Sapphira lied about these things, it showed the depth of the darkness in their minds. The lying done by these individuals was darkness in them and had reached such a point that Satan had infiltrated their hearts.

I John 1:5–6:

This then is the message which we have heard of him, and declare unto you, that God is light, and in him is no darkness at all. If we say that we have fellowship with him, and walk in darkness, we lie, and do not the truth:

Lying is a form of darkness. This couple's lying stood out amid the purity and light of the fellowship of believers noted in Acts 4. Christ in each believer provided the light of life (John 8:12). Had this issue of lying gone unchecked, the purity and light in the fellowship would have been negatively affected. And this would have hindered any future *homothumadon* efforts. Darkness in anyone's life is unfruitful in terms of the things of God and results in things like lying. Christians are not to share in such negative results but rather share in common the light of Christ.

Ephesians 5:11–14:

And have no fellowship with the unfruitful works of darkness, but rather reprove *them*.

For it is a shame even to speak of those things which are done of them in secret.

But all things that are reproved are made manifest by the light: for whatsoever doth make manifest is light.

Wherefore he saith, Awake thou that sleepest, and arise from the dead, and Christ shall give thee light.

Peter addressed the issue as God guided him. The couple was called out, each one separately, and was provided with a choice to change, ". . . from darkness to light, and from the power of Satan unto God . . ." (Acts 26:18). Each had a choice: to leave behind the darkness of Satan and move ahead into the glorious light of the knowledge of the Son of God and the new birth. They were being offered the faith of Christ for salvation (Acts 17:31). However, they both chose the darkness of Satan that had filled their hearts rather than the light of Christ. In this case, this choice produced an immediate negative impact, and they both died.

Acts 5:11–12:

And great fear [respect] came upon all the church, and upon as many as heard these things.

And by the hands of the apostles were many signs and wonders wrought among the people; (and they were all with one accord [*homothumadon*] in Solomon's porch.

This conflict from within the church underscores the idea of *homothumadon* involving a personal conviction in the heart of every person. It is necessary to produce one passion, one mind. Great respect was engendered in every soul. This one accord demonstrated by the believers certainly was conspicuous to those around them. Such one accord was hard to miss because it was not only genuine but also an inspiration for others to join.

Acts 5:13–16:

And of the rest durst no man join himself to them [none from outside the church attempted a similar infiltration as Ananias and Sapphira]: but the people magnified them [this even got the attention of others].

And believers were the more added to the Lord, multitudes both of men and women.)

Insomuch that they brought forth the sick into the streets, and laid them on beds and couches, that at the least the shadow of Peter passing by might overshadow some of them.

There came also a multitude out of the cities round about unto Jerusalem, bringing sick folks, and them which were vexed [to harass, with crowds or tumults—uproars] with unclean spirits: and they were healed everyone.

Everyone who believed for deliverance was healed and even those who had evil spirits (that specialize in mob and crowd harassment) were healed. Such power is accessible and needed today when many are "vexed" via social media assaults. The intimidation many endure through attacks on social media often has malevolent spiritual power behind it. This can be especially true when Satan-led forces suppress free expression of thought and exchange of ideas. Evil becomes emboldened through anonymity and finds momentum not in the character and merit of ideas through reason and commons sense, but in the suppression of any opposition. Often even the idea promoted is only a facade. Control of the conversation is the goal and drives the agenda. Social media can be the few portrayed as the many. Those few can be relentless and levy a heavy penalty of intimidation. Such control of ideas is the tactic of top-down leadership whether they are organized conventionally or unconventionally, whether they have been institutionalized in culture for years or are improvised on the spot as an ad hoc mob. The aim is the same, control through intimidation and fear.

Here we see a one-accord response of respect as the conflict from within was handled. There was great respect in the church, so signs and wonders followed. The expectation in God among the believers was so high that it overwhelmed the adversary and his hold on people. The spirits were removed from influencing and enslaving their lives. The adversary's hold was broken, and everyone was healed! Such power is not only possible today but is truly what is needed. It begins with Christian leaders who do not compromise on their God-given calling.

Sixth Positive Occurrence

We've seen in the first three occurrences of "one accord" a setting of the practical foundation for Christian activity in the community. We have seen in the fourth occurrence a conflict from outside of the church and how they responded by speaking the Word boldly, thereby allowing God's power to be demonstrated. In the fifth occurrence, we saw conflict from within the church, which again was handled with the power of God. As a result, great respect ensued with signs and wonders, and Satan was thwarted.

The sixth occurrence is in Acts 8. It is on the heels of the death of Stephen, one of the seven appointed in Acts 6:5, who challenged the religious hierarchy. Followers of Christ in Jerusalem were being pursued and persecuted. As a result, some reached out with the truth outside of Jerusalem. One man who was also one of the seven, Philip, went down to the city of Samaria and preached Christ. This sixth occurrence documents that the doctrinal and practical foundation set in the context of the first three occurrences of *homothumadon* can be reproduced. One man with a ministry and the heart to serve, aided and guided by God, led a whole city to Christ and into a *homothumadon* experience.

Acts 8:5:

Then Philip went down to the city of Samaria, and preached Christ unto them.

He didn't preach Jesus, he preached "Christ," which reflects the exalted position and title of the Son of God and the divine power latent within his name. Jesus Christ embodies both components of his dual lineage as the Son of God, divine in nature and power, and Son of man, human and subject to suffering and death. His name "Jesus" appearing alone emphasizes all the agony and challenges of mankind and how to handle them with great compassion and empathy. We see Jesus on the cross taking all the sin and suffering of mankind and offering his life as the ultimate payment to atone for these things. Christ, as the anointed of God, emphasizes all the positive expectations of man, culminating in the Christians' glory at the return of Christ (Romans 8:18).

We see in Christ's resurrection that death itself was conquered. He opened the door for believers to follow him into eternal life. We too now have a dual lineage in Adam and also in Christ. In Christ's resurrection was sealed the impending doom and destruction of God's archenemy, Satan, the Devil. Combining the name and the title, we see that "Jesus Christ" embodies the scope of man's spiritual life and future.

Indeed, when the name of Jesus Christ is spoken from a faith-filled heart, it unleashes the impact of the accomplished work of God's only begotten Son, which is "Far above all principality, and power, and might, and dominion, and every name that is named, not only in this world, but also in that which is to come" (Ephesians 1:21).

Acts 8:6–8:

And the people with one accord [*homothumadon*] gave heed unto those things which Philip spake, hearing and seeing the miracles which he did.

For unclean spirits, crying with loud voice, came out of many that were possessed with them: and many taken with palsies, and that were lame, were healed.

And there was great joy in that city.

In this context is yet another movement of God. This is the first Scripture reference of the one-accord concept noted outside of the Jerusalem area. What this means is that the one passion, the one accord, the unity of purpose noted among the apostles and disciples in Jerusalem early in the first-century church can be taught and repeated anywhere and at any time in the Age of Grace.

Remember, the first three occurrences laid the foundation, the fourth occurrence was a conflict from *without*, and the fifth occurrence was a practical conflict from *within*. Here we see the building of another positive foundation. Philip set the proper spiritual foundation (I Corinthians 3:11) that he had learned as recorded in Acts 2, and this brought the same godly results to people.

That's why it's so important to dig deep and get back to that same vein of gold in the Word that God first initiated with the apostles in Acts 2 and revealed further to the Apostle Paul in his epistles regarding the household of faith in the Christian community. Within this knowledge and wisdom are those golden nuggets previously buried under tons of religious rituals, dogma, and commandments of men. We want to tap into this knowledge and wisdom. Collectively, we do this with a *homothumadon*, one-passion effort. Leaders set the spiritual pace and moral example, with each individual believer adding their personal conviction.

Seventh Positive Occurrence

The seventh and final positive occurrence of *homothumadon* in Acts is in Chapter 15 where there is a doctrinal conflict from within the church (please see Chapter 2). The number seven is interesting when studying the significance of numbers used in Scripture. The number seven represents spiritual perfection. In Hebrew, "seven" comes from the root word *savah,* meaning "to be full or satisfied, have enough of." This last occurrence in the Book of Acts culminates the record of the Christian experience with the one-accord concept. With this record, we have a full and satisfactory representation for the Christian church of the grace of God in Christ Jesus. Whether laying a foundation for the Christian walk or dealing with a conflict from within *or* without the church, these seven records form a critical component in what it means to move forward with God's grace and keep the faith . . . anywhere . . . at any time . . . until the return of Christ.

In this seventh positive occurrence, we read about the effort of some to return to works as opposed to grace. To resolve this issue, God moved within leaders, and they came together with the church in Jerusalem. The collective response, with the apostles and elders and brethren present, was deciding how to respond to the problem with one accord. That means there was personal conviction and energy from everyone behind this unity of purpose.

Acts 15:23–25:

And they wrote *letters* by them after this manner; The apostles [plural; God's gifts of service endorsed these letters] and elders and brethren *send* greeting unto the brethren which are of the Gentiles in Antioch and Syria and Cilicia:

Forasmuch as we have heard, that certain which went out from us have troubled [*tarassō*—agitated with various emotions] you with words, subverting your souls, saying, Ye *must* be circumcised, and keep the law: to whom we gave no *such* commandment:

It seemed good unto us, being assembled with one accord [*homothumadon*], to send chosen men unto you with our beloved Barnabas and Paul.

Look at the endorsement that came from this gathering. They were with one accord. We don't know how long it took for them to get to that one passion, but it certainly ended up in one accord. This is the last positive occurrence of *homothumadon* in the Book of Acts. There were possibly many people who had input, but they all came together with one passion, one mind, one heart, and one voice to respond with the appropriate God-guided action.

It is curious that this is the last positive use of *homothumadon* in Acts. As we noted in Chapter 2, the contrast between Acts 15 and Acts 21 is astonishing. By Acts 21, a strong current of Judean-led legalism had swept believers in Jerusalem away from God's grace. Both the knowledge of the household faith (family) and the Body of Christ (function) in the Christian community were disregarded. The apostles are not mentioned as having endorsed the activities of Acts 21. Their absence speaks very loudly.

Christianity has been wrestling with works-versus-grace ever since. By works I mean man-made forms of spirituality issuing from the commandments of men that often involve required rituals, formulaic activity, or practices in attempts to be accepted of God. This as opposed to grace which would be to take the accomplished work of Christ as one's own to be accepted of God.

Finally, there is one more occurrence of *homothumadon* left to consider in Romans 15, and it is the only occurrence in any of the Apostle Paul's writings.

One Occurrence in Romans

This eighth and last occurrence of *homothumadon* magnifies its true God-inspired nature for all to see. Such a one-accord endeavor can only be accomplished while partnering with God. It is appropriate that this last occurrence is found in Romans, the written foundation for Christian doctrine.

Romans 15:4–6:

For whatsoever things were written aforetime were written for our learning, that we through patience and comfort of the scriptures might have hope.

Now the God of patience [endurance, of which hope is the basis] and consolation [a calling near, a summons to one's side . . . encouraging] grant you to be likeminded one toward another according to Christ Jesus:

That ye may with one mind [*homothumadon*] and one mouth glorify God, even the Father of our Lord Jesus Christ.

We need the God of endurance to hold us up under any pressure. Hope is the proper foundation for true endurance in this life. We need the God of encouragement to bring us support, relief, and comfort to help us accomplish our one accord, one passion. He gave us "Christ in you, the hope of glory" (Colossians 1:27), so we already know that only glory awaits us in the future. The God of endurance and encouragement is the strength behind our strength and the reassurance behind our comfort. For us to move together with Him, God will provide the elements of endurance and encouragement that we need to succeed.

What are we to do in this partnership? We are to "be likeminded one toward another [reciprocally, mutually] according to Christ Jesus" to the end we glorify God! So, a genuine *homothumadon* will result in glory to God. All the effort on our part is worthwhile to accomplish this endeavor.

The words "be likeminded" in verse 5 are translated from three Greek words that when put together mean "to think the same thing."

As we take a deeper look at the meaning of this idea "to think the same thing," translated "be likeminded," we find it is used in Philippians.

Philippians 2:2–5:

Fulfil ye my joy, that ye be likeminded, having the same love, *being* of one accord, of one mind.

Let nothing *be done* through strife or vainglory; but in lowliness of mind let each esteem other better than themselves. Look not every man on his own things, but every man also on the things of others.

Let this mind be in you, which was also in Christ Jesus.

The words "be likeminded" in verse two are translated from the same three Greek words as "be likeminded" in Romans 15:5. What is it "to think the same thing?" It is having the mind of Christ (I Corinthians 2:16), having the thoughts of Christ, especially his love. This is how we get like-minded. How is this carried out practically? It is done one toward another according to Christ Jesus.

This "one toward another" from Romans 15:5 in the Greek conveys a meaning of "reciprocally or mutually." Reciprocally or mutually, we are to have the same mind regarding Christ Jesus. It's Christ in each of us! We are to view our fellow brothers and sisters as having the same "measure of faith" of Jesus Christ (Romans 12:3) and the same access to God's grace (Roman 5:1 and 2) and having "Christ in you" (Colossians 1:27).

We are to consistently keep in mind the very nature of God in Christ is in each of us, and that we are a spiritual family. I am not to consider my brother's occupation first, his race, his place of birth, his education, his career, or his address as a filter that screens or squeezes out Christ in my eyes. My brother's identity is the same as mine, a son of God with Christ inside. How powerful is this message? Would seeing my brother's true identity in Christ change how we interact with each other? Absolutely! And it is right in the context of being of one accord.

What should this one accord result be? It should be that with one mind and one mouth we glorify God, even the Father of our Lord Jesus Christ. The result of a genuine *homothumadon* action is to give glory to God for all He has done for us and in us through Christ.

Jeremiah 9:23–24:

Thus saith the LORD, Let not the wise *man* glory in his wisdom, neither let the mighty *man* glory in his might, let not the rich *man* glory in his riches:

But let him that glorieth glory in this, that he understandeth and knoweth me, that I am the LORD which exercise lovingkindness, judgment, and righteousness, in the earth: for in these things I delight, saith the LORD.

Worldly things that are glorified in this life end with men. God moves according to His Word in the hearts of His people in a different direction that begins and ends with Him. When we move with God and His Word, our lives will be a glory to God.

Romans 11:36:

For of him, and through him, and to him, are all things: to whom be glory forever. Amen.

God is the prime mover, the sustainer, and the end of all matters. Every individual has free will and the God-given right to exercise principles initiated by God. Men choose the world's path to their own glory or the path of God's Word to His glory. This choice is the crux of the Christian leadership dilemma. Life becomes simpler when people recognize who is getting the glory from their actions: God or men.

Back in Romans 15, there is more to learn about the true marvel of a *homothumadon* movement of God.

Romans 15:1:
> We then that are strong ought to bear the infirmities of the weak, and not to please ourselves.

The strong here refers to being strong in faith and is contrasted with Romans 14. Read together, these chapters provide great understanding.

Romans 14:1:
> Him that is weak in the faith receive ye, but not to doubtful disputations.

"Weak" does not mean someone is a weak person but weak in the faith or lacking strength in the faith of Jesus Christ or his accomplished work. This is someone who has not grasped grace enough to gain its strength. The weak are still growing and at the point of thinking there is something left for them to do or abstain from to complete faith. This is what the Lord told the Apostle Paul. True strength is in God's grace that is found in the power of Christ.

II Corinthians 12:9:
> And he said unto me, My grace is sufficient for thee: for my strength is made perfect in weakness. Most gladly therefore will I rather glory in my infirmities that the power of Christ may rest upon me.

Romans 14 speaks about how the strong are not to place stumbling blocks in a brother's way, with their freedom in Christ, while others need to discover this freedom for themselves. The strong of Romans 15 are those who know there is nothing to add to or abstain from to complete the work of Christ. So, we are not to judge one another while each of us discovers for ourselves our freedom from works in Christ.

The word "ought" in Romans 15:1 is often used for something that is owed, like money, but here it is used as a metaphor for "goodwill due," like a moral obligation.

There are financial obligations in the Word and there are moral obligations. This is a moral obligation for those who are strong in the faith to bear the infirmities of the weak, those with little strength, and are not to please themselves. The strong who seek to please themselves at their brother's expense do not give glory to God.

Christ did not place his own feelings about his impending suffering above the need of mankind to be spiritually rescued (Matthew 26:36–44). In order to accomplish man's redemption, he followed God's will. Jesus Christ is the best example of not pleasing himself.

Romans 15:2–3:

Let every one of us please his neighbour for his good to edification [to build each other up].

For even Christ pleased not himself; but, as it is written, The reproaches of them that reproached thee fell on me.

Becoming part of a genuine *homothumadon* endeavor involves believing in something greater than ourselves, the purposes and will of God. To be part of such a movement of God brings each believer face-to-face with selfless service that is immersed in the purposes and will of God. Such a unique adventure is exciting to the soul that trusts in God. Not every detail is known, not every aspect mapped out, yet there is a confidence and assurance to move ahead, knowing that we partner with God who guides us to success and victory.

We have seen seven positive occurrences of *homothumadon* in Acts and one in Romans. In the context of each occurrence in Acts, there is a movement of God that inspired this unity of purpose and action among believers. God moves and works within His children who have a mindset of serving one another in love. It is such a movement of God that inspires the setting of the foundation of His Word for others to build upon. It is such a movement of God that inspires answers, solutions, and guidance in response to conflict or challenges from within or without the Christian community and local fellowship.

It is leaders—those who take the initiative to move with God—who set the spiritual pace and right moral example for others to follow. They do so with the energy of their own conviction, regardless of whether they have titles or not. Such leaders serve, help the joy, and are the example to follow so others too can add their own personal conviction, enthusiasm, and commitment to such a movement.

I Corinthians 3:7–9:

So then neither is he that planteth anything, neither he that watereth; but God that giveth the increase.

Now he that planteth and he that watereth are one: and every man shall receive his own reward according to his own labour. For we are labourers together with God: ye are God's husbandry, *ye are* God's building.

We each can plant and water the Word of Life in the hearts of people, but only God causes that seed to grow. We labor together with God as He moves. Together with Him, we build a *homothumadon* effort to establish and reaffirm the foundation for the Christian walk.

I Corinthians 3:10–11:

According to the grace of God which is given unto me, as a wise masterbuilder, I have laid the foundation, and another buildeth thereon. But let every man take heed how he buildeth thereupon.

For other foundation can no man lay than that is laid, which is Jesus Christ.

Jesus Christ is highlighted in the first three occurrences of *homothumadon* in the Book of Acts. The believers followed his instructions; they took ownership and used the gift of the holy spirit offered to them after his ascension. Then believers freely joined themselves to this new community based on what Christ accomplished for them and in them. The Book of Acts is an ongoing account of how the first Christians developed individually and as a community based on this foundation. Their knowledge and application of the truth regarding Christ continued to grow on a personal level and it spread to other lands and people.

Whether laying a foundation for the Christian walk or dealing with a conflict from within or without the church, God continues to move to help His people. Our privilege and responsibility as believers are to respond to God as He moves in us and with us. Such responses begin with leaders—those who take the initiative to move with God—and then everyone adds their own personal conviction in one accord.

In conclusion, the question to ask yourself at this moment is, "What is God moving in my life?" Then ask a second question, "What am I going to do about it?" The prayer of the faithful in Christ is that you respond to Him.

Chapter 4

A CHRISTIAN MINISTRY AND
THE HOUSEHOLD OF FAITH

I t is a revelation to many people to discover that any individual Christian ministry or church is not the complete embodiment of the household of faith as described in the Bible. God's family or household is an arrangement of His design and is not of man. God places no difference between man-made distinctions such as denominational groups in terms of their names or histories or locations. So, in this chapter, we will consider the truth regarding a Christian ministry and how it relates to the household of faith. We will see that a Christian ministry and the household of faith are not one and the same, but clearly separate and distinct. Then we will see how it relates to our overall understanding of what it means to give an answer of truth in the face of accusations leveled by resistant authorities or powers.

The Christian ministry, simply stated, involves all service and labor performed on behalf of Christ that lines up with God's Word. The real key is keeping the right heart or attitude in service; otherwise, we become self-absorbed, and God and His Word are not involved. The attitude with which we serve is always paramount: Are we selfless or selfish, Christ-centered, or self-centered in our service?

When we are selfless, or Christ-centered, our thankful and cheerful heart is in our giving. This is profitable, producing good fruit, and it results in godly service. When we are self-absorbed and self-serving, service becomes obligatory and religious. Comparisons and accusations result. This is unprofitable and produces bad fruit. Let's look at an example of this in Luke 10.

Service: Jesus, Martha, and Mary

Luke 10:38–42:

Now it came to pass, as they went, that he [Jesus] entered into a certain village: and a certain woman named Martha received him into her house.

And she had a sister called Mary, which also sat at Jesus' feet, and heard his word.

But Martha was cumbered about much serving [*diakonia*], and came to him, and said, Lord, dost thou not care that my sister hath left me to serve alone? bid her therefore that she help me.

And Jesus answered and said unto her, Martha, Martha, thou art careful and troubled about many things:

But one thing is needful: and Mary hath chosen that good part, which shall not be taken away from her.

There is tremendous learning here regarding service. The word "serving" in verse 40 is translated from the Greek word *diakonia*. *Diakonia* simply means "service, ministering, esp. of those who execute the commands of others," which can be as basic as serving food (like here) or labor on behalf of the cause of Christ to make known the gospel. This account is uniquely significant and stands out to us because Luke is the only gospel of the four that records this account.

Martha was cumbered about with much serving. "Cumbered" here means "to be distracted, overly occupied with cares or business." As a result, Martha accused Jesus by saying, "Lord, dost thou not care . . .?" Of course, Jesus cared! He always did his Father's will and walked in love. She not only accused Jesus of not caring, but she also accused Mary, saying, "My sister hath left me alone."

After Martha accused Mary, she began directing the lives of others. She commanded Jesus to have her sister help her. The Greek grammatical construction of the word for "bid" is an urgent command directed toward Jesus Christ. Commanding people to perform service is a habit to be avoided. People begin to resent being commanded when it is not appropriate or warranted. Without the right heart of service, or freely giving of oneself, bad fruit results.

Self-absorbed service, though it appears pious, drives the work but loses the heart, just like Martha did in commanding Jesus. The heart of Christian service is tied to remembering "I serve the Lord." We can get so involved with service that we forget why we are serving and on whose behalf we serve. Martha had forgotten the Lord in her service. Jesus Christ addressed Martha's attitude, not service itself. He said, "Martha, Martha, thou art careful and troubled about many things." "Careful" means "to be anxious about" and indicates a distracted mind about many things. Jesus Christ said, "But one thing is needful: and Mary hath chosen that good part."

The greatest example of service we have is Jesus Christ. Just as God provides meaning and purpose to our lives, Jesus Christ shows how to live out that meaning and purpose. Here, Jesus helped Martha by teaching her, "Mary hath chosen that good part." Mary made a good choice.

This brings up a simple point about service. We are not victims—we choose. Romans 8 tells us we are not to be sheep led to the slaughter, but we are more than conquerors through Him that loved us (Romans 8:36–37). A more-than-a-conqueror mindset is a response to God and His love. Victimization is often a rejection of God's involvement when we are pressured, and it leads to becoming self-absorbed like Martha in this record.

Mary, however, chose the good part. What did she choose? She "sat at Jesus' feet and heard his word" (Luke 10:39). The Word is the good part. The Word is how we grow in our knowledge of God. Jesus Christ embodied the purest expression of the Word and heart of God. In other words, what Jesus said and did was what God wanted to be said and done in each situation. This is the good part Martha left out. As we read this section, we see how the Word of God shows us how to give ourselves freely in service.

Let me clearly point out that there is everything right with service when people can honestly handle it and avoid anxiety about serving. That is why in Christian service the Word must be first and central. Because the Word believed produces the right fruit—not the bad fruit of anxiety, which results in a distracted mind and victimization, prompting accusations against others. Perhaps what Martha should have done when she realized she was getting anxious is simply put the "pots and pans" aside and listen. The good thing to choose is what is the priority in the moment. Many would consider it a priority being with Jesus while he was in your home. When we are self-absorbed, we often miss the priority though it may be right in front of us.

This clear distinction is a lesson that applies to the individual and, in a broader sense, to any activity or work of a Christian ministry. We will see this further in the first occurrence of *diakonia* in the Book of Acts.

The Foundation for Service in Acts

Acts 1:14–17:

These all continued with one accord in prayer and supplication, with the women, and Mary the mother of Jesus, and with his brethren.

And in those days Peter stood up in the midst of the disciples, and said, (the number of names together were about an hundred and twenty,)

Men and brethren, this scripture must needs have been fulfilled, which the Holy Ghost by the mouth of David spake before concerning Judas, which was guide to them that took Jesus.

For he was numbered with us, and had obtained part of this ministry [*diakonia*].

Here Peter spoke of needing another to fill a part of the ministry that Judas left vacant when he went and hanged himself. The word "part" in verse 17 can be rendered "allotted portion." There was an allotted portion of the ministry needing to be filled by someone with the right credentials.

What is this ministry that is spoken of here? Jesus had given the apostles final instructions before departing into heaven. In Jesus' absence, the disciples carried out his teaching and instruction. Everything Jesus had taught and instructed them provided the basis for the fledgling ministry to develop into what we know today as Christianity

Acts 1:20–22:

For it is written in the book of Psalms, Let his habitation be desolate, and let no man dwell therein: and his bishoprick let another take.

Wherefore of these men which have companied with us all the time that the Lord Jesus went in and out among us,

Beginning from the baptism of John, unto that same day that he was taken up from us, must one be ordained to be a witness with us of his resurrection.

The context shows that Word-based decisions are part of a Christian ministry. They went right to the Word that was accessible to them. Here they considered two separate Psalms in the Old Testament to get their understanding. Someone must have understood these verses to be able to apply them correctly to this situation. "It is written" is the standard upon which we function in a Christian ministry or local church. The written Word and the example of Jesus Christ were central in the decision to fill this part of the ministry left empty by Judas.

"In and out among us" from verse 21 is a Hebrew expression used to convey official actions or life in general. Often it is applied to exercising leadership among the people. The apostles focused on the time frame from John's baptism all the way through the ascension, or the whole time they had access to Jesus while he was on earth. That was important to them. They had Jesus Christ in person as an example. He was the Word made flesh, the embodiment of God's will. Everything that he did was according to the Word. One great key in developing leaders is exposure to other leaders in as many situations as possible. Learning in real-life scenarios is vital to spiritual development.

Today, putting on the mind of Christ through the Word of God is how we can be followers of Christ in his absence (Romans 13:14; I

Corinthians 2:16). We walk in love and in the "newness of life" (Romans 6:4) offered to us by God in Christ. We don't have Jesus in person to help, but we do have the recorded examples in the Word. We also have the living examples of seasoned believers and ministers around us to help us learn how to carry out the work of the ministry.

Acts 1:24–26:
And they prayed, and said, Thou, Lord, which knowest the hearts of all men, shew whether of these two thou hast chosen,

That he may take part of this ministry [*diakonia*] and apostleship, from which Judas by transgression fell, that he might go to his own place.

And they gave forth their lots; and the lot fell upon Matthias; and he was numbered with the eleven apostles.

We are each to take our part, or our "allotted portion," of this ministry on behalf of Christ. We can see three characteristics of this word *diakonia* in the context of this section of Scripture where it is first used in Acts. This helps us gain a biblical understanding of the ministry and recognize these characteristics as they appear in the Scriptures.

1. Jesus Christ is central to the ministry. His example, teaching, and instruction were what the disciples used to launch their Christian service on his behalf. Since we no longer have Christ here to instruct us personally, in his absence we are given the "comforter" or the holy spirit and the name of Jesus Christ (John 14-16), which embodies his accomplished work, explained in the "all truth" (John 16:13) as noted in the writings of the Apostle Paul and others as the faith of Jesus Christ (Romans 3:22). We have the mind of Christ (1 Corinthians 2:16) that we might walk in love and newness of life (Romans 6:4) and carry

out the works Christ did and greater as we work together (John 14:12). This is the foundation of Christian service.

2. A Word-based approach to the Christian ministry is vital. The Word must be the basis of every decision, every activity, every program, and every labor or service that's performed on behalf of Christ. Personal opinions and experiences may or may not line up with Scripture and should be vetted accordingly.

3. The Christian ministry is portioned out. No one person does everything—it is a team approach, like parts of the human body. Therefore, an organized approach fits well so individual strengths can flourish. This includes leaders like apostles, prophets, evangelists, pastors, and teachers (Ephesians 4:11) and "helps and governments" (I Corinthians 12:28).

Building Upon the Foundation of Service in Acts

The next two occurrences of *diakonia* in Acts are in Chapter 6. Here we see the developing concept of the Christian ministry as the church grew.

Acts 6:1:

And in those days, when the number of the disciples was multiplied, there arose a murmuring of the Grecians against the Hebrews, because their widows were neglected in the daily ministration [*diakonia*].

The ministry or service at that time was not adequate to meet the rising needs. Many of the devout who had come from around the world to attend the feast of Pentecost (a one-day feast) just stayed in Jerusalem, and the service structure was not adequate to reach everyone. The team of twelve apostles was not large enough and further "portioning" of the ministry was needed.

Acts 6:2:

Then the twelve called the multitude of the disciples *unto them*, and said, It is not reason that we should leave the word of God, and serve [*diakoneō* verb form of *diakonia*] tables.

The word "reason" is particularly important to understanding this verse. The English Standard Version of the Bible renders this word "right." Further, the word "reason" is translated from a Greek word that means "pleasing to God, and therefore, proper, fitting, in His sight." The apostles were *willing* to perform those tasks, such as serving tables, but it wasn't pleasing, nor was it *right* to God to leave the Word. Teaching and ministering the Word is service and must lead the Christian ministry. We see this truth written by the Apostle Paul in Ephesians Chapter 4.

Ephesians 4:11–12:

And he gave some, apostles; and some, prophets; and some, evangelists; and some, pastors and teachers;

For the perfecting of the saints, for the work of the ministry, for the edifying of the body of Christ.

The number one purpose of apostles, prophets, evangelists, pastors, and teachers—men and women called of God as gifts to serve others—is to perfect the saints. Without this service, the work of the ministry and the edifying of the Body of Christ cannot function as God designed it. There would be lack.

It is incumbent upon those who serve in the Body of Christ to be examples in character by setting solid ethical standards that they themselves live. Lack of biblical character is at the heart of the Christian leadership dilemma. Solid ethical behavior is perhaps one of the most impacting and transformational elements of perfecting the saints these moral agents provide. The best examples for others to follow are those whose words line up with their actions without hypocrisy. It is only upon the grace of God in Christ Jesus that such ethical examples and the successful perfecting of the saints are accomplished (I Peter 5:10).

The saints are perfected in the sense of "making fully ready… perfectly equipping and fully preparing" them in their newness-of-life walk which includes standards of what is right from God's perspective and not the world. It is a new life, so learning how to live it necessitates help from others who can show us the right moral example.

These men and women called of God are those building and restorative agents—servants, helpers of the believers' joy, and examples in word and deed—to help us. They are to take the initiative to move with God, set the spiritual pace, and be the right moral example. Then the work of the ministry can build from there.

Service in Christ is truly organic and springs forth when the saints have their needs met. The heartbeat of a child of God sends life-giving purpose, satisfaction, and strength to them in service. Jesus Christ is the greatest example for us to follow. As the work of the ministry develops, individual strengths emerge naturally within the body of believers, which produces the third part, "for the edifying of the body of Christ." This is the environment in which individual strengths emerge, which build others in love.

Acts 6:3:

Wherefore, brethren, look ye out among you seven men of honest report, full of the Holy Ghost and wisdom, whom we may appoint over this business.

The word "full" is an adjective describing the "men" to be chosen. "Full" can also mean complete or sufficient. So here are the criteria for the right candidates to be considered among the Christian community to fill this job position: "full, complete, or sufficient" in "the Holy Ghost and wisdom." There is no mention of what they looked like, the color of their skin, how tall they were, their talents, personalities, education, age, or any other social standard someone might think to apply. When too much focus is placed on the *outside*, what really goes unnoticed is what really matters, what people have on the *inside*. What a lesson!

The words "Holy Ghost [holy spirit] and wisdom" are key to understanding this verse. These words grouped together are the figure of speech *hendiadys*, which means "Two words employed, but only one thing, or idea intended." So, combining "Holy Ghost [holy spirit]" with "wisdom," it can be rendered "holy spirit wisdom" or "spiritual wisdom." They needed someone who was full, not of their own wisdom or man's wisdom, but full of the wisdom that comes from God. This is a wonderful criterion to include when choosing leadership.

I Corinthians 2:5–7:

That your [the] faith [household faith[15]] should not stand in the wisdom of men, but in the power of God.

Howbeit we speak wisdom among them that are perfect [mature]: yet not the wisdom of this world, nor of the princes of this world, that come to nought:

But we speak the *wisdom* of God in a mystery, *even* the hidden *wisdom*, which God ordained before the world unto our glory:

This spiritual wisdom—the hidden newness-of-life walk in Christ that can only be spiritually discerned (I Corinthians 2:8–16)—is a wonderful characteristic to look for while encouraging leaders to the work of the ministry. This spiritual wisdom is applied by those who stand on the faith of Jesus Christ—his accomplished work of redemption that

---

15 The household faith (Galatians 6:10) is the common faith (Titus 1:4) of Jesus Christ that all Christians share as brothers and sisters in the family of God.

provides the payment by which the gift of holy spirit was offered to man through grace.

The Ministry and Business

Acts 6:3:

Wherefore, brethren, look ye out among you seven men of honest report, full of the Holy Ghost and wisdom, whom we may appoint over this business.

There is a business side to running a Christian ministry, a local church, or home fellowship, but the ministry, a local church, or a home fellowship are not to be businesses. The word "business" in verse 3 is defined by *Thayer's Greek-English Lexicon of the New Testament* on page 671 as "duty or business." The context here clearly refers to taking care of people's physical needs, so this "business" is, indeed, part of the Christian ministry or other local groups. When physical needs are not met, people may become distracted from the Word and their fellowship with other believers can be hindered. Christian service takes into consideration the physical, mental, and spiritual needs of people.

Acts 6:4

But we will give ourselves continually to prayer, and to the ministry [*diakonia*] of the word.

This section of Acts shows that some people are called and excel in contributing by serving God's Word and spiritual needs (I Timothy 1:3; 4:13–16), while others are called and excel in caring for physical or practical needs. All these efforts are necessary for the Christian community to thrive. This section is not about making distinctions in how people serve, as if one is better than another, but rather pinpointing the Word as the catalyst that ignites the engine of the Christian experience and ministry. Both have their place. As in the lesson of Martha, there may be other priorities, like the Word, we should consider instead of allowing ourselves to get anxious while we serve. The Word of God is to be given merited attention.

Today the work of the Christian ministry might be more involved than in the first century because of legal demands, regulations, and cultural conditions. But the biblical distinction of serving the "bread of life" as the priority and "serving bread," or meeting physical needs, is present. This is the biblical pattern to follow.

Anyone who has served in some capacity in the Christian community understands that the care of physical needs is an important consideration. The range of these physical needs varies. This may include having an adequate amount of water, shelter, or food. Jesus Christ understood this very well. In Mark 6:34–44, he taught and fed "about five thousand." He made sure their physical hunger was satisfied so that they could have their spiritual hunger satisfied. Each situation should be evaluated individually to have God's best solution for people.

Acts 6:5:
> And the saying pleased the whole multitude . . .

The word translated "pleased" here is the verb form of the same word used in verse 2, which was translated "reason," meaning pleasing to God or "right." When something pleases God, or is proper and fitting in His sight, it will be right and fit for those who believe God. This may not be true for those who just believe *in* God. Many people believe *in* God, meaning they are aware of and acknowledge His existence. But those who believe God, take it a step further. They take Him at His Word by acting on His revealed Word. Faith is simply to believe God.

Stephen is an example of someone who believed God and stood on the accomplished work of Christ.

A Man Full of Holy Spirit Faith

Clearly, the work of the ministry follows the Word being served to the believers. It is the environment where individual strengths develop. These emerging, well-fitted strengths in service are exactly what happened here in verse 5 with the example of Stephen.

Acts 6:5:

And the saying pleased the whole multitude: and they chose Stephen, a man full of faith and of the Holy Ghost, and Philip, and Prochorus, and Nicanor, and Timon, and Parmenas, and Nicolas a proselyte of Antioch.

In verse 5, we again see the figure of speech *hendiadys* (two words used for one idea) regarding Stephen. He was a man "full of faith and of the Holy Ghost [holy spirit]." The word "full" once more means "full, complete, or sufficient" and reflects the man, Stephen. According to this figure of speech, he is described as a man full of holy spirit faith. Holy spirit faith is referring to the faith of Jesus Christ that came with the gift of holy spirit. This faith is the accomplished work of Christ who believed God every step of his life to complete our redemption when he declared these words on the cross, "It is finished" (John 19:30).

Hebrews 12:2:

Looking unto Jesus the author and finisher [or "founder and perfecter" in ESV] of *our* [the] faith; who for the joy that was set before him endured the cross, despising the shame, and is set down at the right hand of the throne of God.

Full of holy spirit faith, or the faith of Jesus Christ, describes Stephen's willingness to rely on the work of another man, his savior Jesus Christ. Jesus Christ is the founder and perfecter of the faith given to us by God for justification (Romans 3:22–24; Galatians 2:16). It is this faith that God energizes (I Corinthians 12:9) to bring about the works of Christ (John 14:12) and greater works. We as sons of God can work in harmony with other children of God (the Body of Christ), something Jesus could not do because this truth had not yet been offered to man. Stephen would have been in the category of being strong in the faith (Romans 15:1).

This is the criteria God inspired within the hearts of the apostles to support the service needed so the Word could continue to live. The apostles made this known, and this pleased everyone. It was a good fit in the hearts of the disciples.

Acts 6:6:

Whom they set before the apostles: and when they had prayed, they laid their hands on them.

The apostles commissioned these chosen men to "this business" that was vital to meeting the physical needs in the church.

The pattern in the Scripture is clear. The Word is the priority when it comes to the work of the ministry as we saw with Jesus, Mary, and Martha in Luke 10. There is a business aspect in service on behalf of Christ, but the ministry is not a business. This truth cannot be overstated. It is the moral imperative for Christian leaders to not allow a business or worldly model to dominate and dictate the affairs of the church.

If a Christian ministry, church, or organization crosses that line and follows a business model, people often find institutionalized hypocrisy, an inflated respect of high-ranking individuals, and the love of money. The environment becomes toxic with each step in this direction. God's

Word becomes a product for sale, people become objects to be used, and proper care for those in need dwindles.

What prevents these negative results is keeping the Word first, above the "business" side of the ministry.

The next verse reveals a safeguard to keep service on the right track: obedience to the household of faith.

Obedience to the Household Faith

Acts 6:7:

> And the word of God increased [it does not say the business side of the ministry increased]; and the number of the disciples multiplied in Jerusalem greatly; and a great company of the priests [Judeans[16]] were obedient to the faith [the household faith].

In this first mention of the household of faith in Acts, God put a safeguard to preserve the heart of the ministry. It is so appropriate that this concept comes up early in Acts. Because as the church transitioned into their newfound access and relationship with God through Christ, they were laying down steppingstones by God's wisdom that other Christians could follow. This is precisely what we are endeavoring to do today as we address the Christian leadership dilemma by moving ahead with grace and keeping the faith.

This fundamental practice of obedience reveals one of the most significant building blocks of grace for the Christian believer. It is the accomplished work of Christ. The achievement of Christ was, without sin or stumbling, to conquer sin and its consequences. Every act and prophetic fulfillment he accomplished on our behalf God has packaged

---

16 "Instead of ἱεϱεων, priests, a few MSS, and the Syriac, read Ιουδαιων, Jews" [Judeans]

and is offering to man. To obey the faith is to accept this work without any merit of our own. That is why obedience to the faith is so important, because our Christian walk does not begin with our work but on the work of another. That is grace. All Christian believers share this common bond of the faith of Jesus Christ as God's children.

The household of faith in Galatians 6:10 is the common faith of Titus 1:4 and the faith of Jesus Christ in Romans 3:22 that we all share as brothers and sisters in the family of God. Acts 6:7 does not say "obedient to the ministry." If God wanted to say that He would have said that. God's Word says, "obedient to the [household] faith."

Biblically, the Christian ministry and the household of faith are not one and the same. A Christian ministry moves within the knowledge of the household faith but never absolutely declares, for example, "Our group exclusively is the true household of faith." The household of faith is framed by truth—it is of God and therefore spiritual, not physical, or manmade.

Acts 6:7 summarizes what had taken place in the fledgling church up to that point as recorded in Acts and as such is a figure of speech that invites further scrutiny. We can refer to Acts 2 to discover what lead to this obedience to the faith. At the onset of the Christian church, the first Christians had mutual respect one for another based on the gift of holy spirit each person received. This gift represented remission of sins and eternal life salvation through grace and not works.

This was a sharp contrast to what these followers of Judaism had known for some 1,400 years, which was the works of the Law to temporarily cover their sins. The epistles of Romans through Thessalonians, written by the Apostle Paul, later revealed the truth behind what was received in the gift of holy spirit. The gospels of Matthew through John show the work of Christ. Romans through Thessalonians explain the work of Christ. The Book of Acts shows the transition between them.

The first practical recognition of how they viewed each other in their new relationships was exhibited in mutual respect.

Acts 2:38,42–43:

Then Peter said unto them [the devout attending the feast of Pentecost who positively responded to the apostles], Repent, and be baptized every one of you in the name of Jesus Christ for the remission of sins, and ye shall receive the gift of the Holy Ghost.

And they continued stedfastly in the apostles' doctrine and fellowship, and in breaking of bread, and in prayers.

And fear [respect] came upon [began and continued upon[17]] every soul: and many wonders and signs were done by the apostles.

Doctrinal truth is the lens by which Christian believers should view each other, not through the lens of denominational differences. This also includes having respect for oneself based on our identity in Christ. This can be difficult for those conditioned by denominational dogma and commandments of men rather than the Word of God.

Mutual Respect

Obedience to the faith begins with mutual respect based on the accomplished work of Christ. This accomplished work can be summed up in one word: grace. The words "came upon" are translated from one Greek word which highlights that this respect had a starting point, implying origin. In addition, its verbal construction denotes continuous action in the past. For us who are keenly interested in how the early Christians conducted themselves, this is a real vein of truth to mine.

---

17 The words "came upon" represent one Greek verb which in its grammatical construction here indicates continuous action in the past.

This Acts 2 scriptural record of Pentecost allows us to see the truth in practice regarding when and how Christianity truly began. Stripped away are all the layers of dogma, misinformation, and commandments of men heaped on it over the years. What remains is pristine and pure like crystal clear water released from a glacier untouched for thousands of years.

This is amazing when we consider the journey and relationship for God's people began some 2,000 years ago with something quite simple: mutual respect.[18] Practically speaking, Christianity is based on mutual respect for what God did for each person in Christ. Mutual respect is not based on socioeconomics, education, bloodline, race, geography, or anything man can do or anything that is passed on through birth. This is not surface respect, but one that is recognized from God's perspective, not man's, which is the value of each soul. This is the basis for mutual respect. It's the cornerstone of how we build our relationships one with another.

The household of faith is built upon valuing the treasure we each have in our earthen vessels (II Corinthians 4:7). It is Christ in you (Colossians 1:27) and it's Christ in me. That means Christ's accomplished work as the ultimate sacrifice for sin provided eternal life for all and the potential to walk like him. All this is embodied in the gift of holy spirit. Wow! Life doesn't get any bigger than that!

Respect for what God did in us through Christ is the basis for mutual Christian respect no matter what group someone affiliates with or joins. This brings up the question, "Do I need to respect everything people decide to do with God's gift of grace?" The answer to this is clearly no. "Do I respect their right to choose?" The answer to this question is clearly yes. We can respect what God has accomplished through Christ in each of us, but that does not mean we then must agree with how each

---

18　The other components to any biblical relationship besides mutual respect are mutual giving and receiving.

child of God decides to live. God loves all men, all the inhabitants of the world, and demonstrated it when He gave His Son to all mankind for salvation.

John 3:16:

For God so loved the world [*kosmos*[19]], that he gave his only begotten Son, that whosoever believeth in him should not perish, but have everlasting life.

However, God does not agree with all man does including His children. The choices man makes that God does not agree with are those in which man has allowed his motives to be influenced and corrupted from something other than God. "The world" can also refer to the Satanic corruption that is in it.

I John 2:15–17:

Love not the world [*kosmos*], neither the things that are in the world [*kosmos*]. If any man love the world [*kosmos*], the love of the Father is not in him.

For all that is in the world [*kosmos*], the lust of the flesh, and the lust of the eyes, and the pride of life, is not of the Father, but is of the world [*kosmos*].

And the world [*kosmos*] passeth away, and the lust thereof: but he that doeth the will of God abideth forever.

Yes, God does not approve of all the acts of men. Loving "not the world, neither the things that are in the world" refers to the acts of men,

---

19 The Greek word *kosmos* translated "world" can mean 1) the ordered universe 2) all the inhabitants living in the ordered universe 3) the portion of Satanically-influenced inhabitants and corrupted systems present in the ordered universe. Context determines which meaning best applies. See endnote for Ethelbert W. Bullinger, pp 900–901.

independent of God, where men choose options that contradict God's purposes, heart, and Word. Any parent can understand that we love our children but may not always approve of their behavior. This is also true with God our Heavenly Father.

God looks on the heart of man, so motives play a key role. Man does incorporate motive when legally adjudicating a matter, but it remains elusive and hard to determine at times. This is not true of God. The Word has plenty to say about what is right and wrong. Yet motives can determine whether a particular action is right or wrong from God's perspective. The fruit of someone's action can be a clear indicator. Motive resides in the heart of everyone and ultimately is between that person and God.

A scenario where motive being key to something being right or wrong might be if you or a loved one were involved in a life-threatening situation, where time was of the essence. In this scenario, there might not be time to explain yourself before you act.

For example, let us say a parent is crossing a road with a child, and the child does not see an oncoming vehicle. The parent grabs the child by the arm and jerks them back onto the sidewalk. No communication, just action.

Yet, to make a habit of jerking the child by the arm is not a healthy practice. Most people would agree that your motive to protect yourself or a loved one from harm overrides all else. Yet, we cannot live in a constant state of such intervening action without ever communicating to anyone. Communication is vital to the health of our interaction.

Often people who are prone to manufacture constant crises where none exist fall prey to action without communication or appropriate dialogue. That would be confusing and wrong as a lifestyle. But in emergency situations, when the only right course is immediate action, intervening to protect life and limb without communication is rightly justified. Such intervention should be unique and atypical. Motive does make a difference.

Christian leaders should be very leery of aligning themselves with any tide of consistent crises that result in taking away the freedom of others, especially the right to choose one's own course in life. A crisis should be properly vetted and rechecked periodically to ensure conditions have or have not changed. Otherwise, draconian type measures of control, if initiated, may remain in place, and continue unchecked even though the crisis has been alleviated.

So respecting others for what God wrought in Christ, not necessarily what they choose to do with it, is our foundation. The mutual respect here in Acts 2 starts with what God has done. Now let us be clear, of course, there was respect among people prior to Acts 2:43. In fact, in the same chapter, verse 5 says that there were devout men from every nation participating in the feast of Pentecost. Calling them "devout" shows that they lived a lifestyle of reverencing God and each other in the context of Judaism. But the respect in verse 43 runs a lot deeper.

The mutual respect we are speaking about began with the understanding that the faith of Jesus Christ bridged the gap between man and God, so each believer received eternal life. By grace, salvation was offered by God. It was not accomplished or given by "devout" behavior. This truth built mutual respect and inspired sharing together to meet needs.

Acts 2:44–46:

And all that believed were together, and had all things common;

And sold their possessions and goods, and parted them to all *men*, as every man had need.

And they, continuing daily with one accord [*homothumadon*]
in the temple, and breaking bread from house to house, did eat
their meat with gladness and singleness of heart,

This was the foundation that was embraced with one accord. The
very first practical step that led to the obedience to the household of faith
was having respect one for another. This is especially important when
it comes to keeping equilibrium in the Christian ministry. My service
is not greater than your service, or vice versa. It is simply different. This
is the basis of understanding the unique functions we each have in the
Body of Christ.

The household faith centers on the same faith of Jesus Christ we
all have in God's family. God is the head of His family as the Father in
relation to the household of faith. Our relationship as children of God
will never cease. It is eternal. The Body of Christ, the church, depends
on the unique functions we each have as members in one body under
one head, Christ. Christ (the emphasis is not on Jesus) is the head of
the Body in relation to how members function together to build it. The
head represents the source of life according to J.D. Douglas (*New Bible
Dictionary*, page 457).

Christ is not directing the affairs of the church, but his accomplished
work is how the life of God flows through the Body. Our functioning
in the Body of Christ, as we know it, will cease at the return of Christ
(Ephesians 4:11–13). Family (same faith) before function (different
function) is a good perspective for the Christian community to embrace.

The Book of Romans is the foundational treatise of the Age of Grace
in which we live. Within Romans, God teaches that obedience to the
faith should be promoted and taught to others. This is the foundation
each Christian believer, new or seasoned, should build upon. God wants
all people of all nations to know these truths.

Romans 1:5:

By whom we have received grace and apostleship, for obedience to the [household] faith among all nations, for his name.

Romans 16:26:

But now is made manifest, and by the scriptures of the prophets, according to the commandment of the everlasting God, made known to all nations for the obedience of [household] faith.

Obedience to the household faith bookends this great revelation in the first and last chapters of Romans. This obedience helps keep the Christian ministry on the right track because it is a mutual respect that is at the foundation of functioning in unity. We all have the same measure of faith but not the same function.

Romans 12:3–5:

For I say, through the grace given unto me, to every man that is among you, not to think *of himself* more highly than he ought to think; but to think soberly, according as God hath dealt to every man the measure of faith [of Jesus Christ].

For as we have many members in one body, and all members have not the same office [function]:

So we, *being* many, are one body in Christ, and every one members one of another.

The practical foundation for the household of faith was first laid out in the Book of Acts. God got the new church off to a good start. And the first practical step in being obedient to the household of faith is mutual respect because God had dealt to every man the measure of faith. This biblical perspective helps to level the playing field for all Christians by justifying all by the same standard—the faith of Jesus Christ. Can you imagine what life would be like if we all began to think this way!

Galatians 2:16:

Knowing that a man is not justified by the works of the law, but by the faith of Jesus Christ, even we have believed in Jesus Christ, that we might be justified by the faith of Christ, and not by the works of the law: for by the works of the law shall no flesh be justified.

Paying close attention to the personal pronouns and individual references in the following verses shows Paul's personal conviction and confession of an identity with Jesus Christ.

Galatians 2:20–21:

I am crucified with Christ [the text reads "I have been crucified with"]: nevertheless, I live; yet not I, but Christ liveth in me: and the life which I now live in the flesh I live by the faith [believing God to accomplish the work] of the Son of God, who loved me, and gave himself for me.

I do not frustrate the grace of God: for if righteousness *come* by the law, then Christ is dead in vain.

The words "I am crucified with," or more precisely, "I have been crucified with" are translated from one Greek verb. This is an indicative perfect tense verb here, which means the action of the crucifixion was conducted in the past, but its significance and impact continue to the present. This truth cannot be overstated, it is in perpetuity. The action of Christ to offer his life on the cross continues to the present. The true Christian identity in Christ, here represented by the Apostle Paul as he refers to himself in the first person, rests clearly upon the crucifixion of the old man[20] with Christ (Romans 6:6).

The belief that Jesus Christ exhibited encompassed his entire sinless life and sacrifice. For Jesus, it was believing God in action to fulfill God's plan. For us, after the fact, it is the faith of Jesus Christ, because he already accomplished God's plan—it is finished. His believing God to the uttermost, his faith, his trust, his assurance, and his confidence in God became to us the faith of Jesus Christ embodying all these things. Therefore, the household of faith is built on mutual respect in what Christ accomplished, which is summed up in the faith of Jesus Christ.

This mutual respect begins with each of us personally. We take Christ's believing as our faith and embrace it with full persuasion, enthusiasm, and commitment. Mutual respect in Christ recognizes and values each other's strengths and potential.

This point is highlighted in Galatians 2:20 and 21, where Paul individually and personally declares his present life is lived through the faith of the Son of God. Jesus' believing action and sacrifice equals the Christian believer's salvation and potential to walk like Christ. Who among us would not respect that! That is why the faith of Christ leads right into recognizing and living the hidden wisdom of God—Christ in each of us and together we make up the Body of Christ. It's brilliant the way God set this up. To believe otherwise is to frustrate the grace of God.

I Corinthians 12:21 states, "And the eye cannot say unto the hand, I have no need of thee: nor again the head to the feet, I have no need of you." For the Body of Christ to function as divinely designed we need each other.

---

20 The "old man" refers to the nature of disobedience handed down from Adam that results in the collected habits of disobedience to God beginning at natural birth, which leads to being "carnally minded," as opposed to the "new man" nature of Christ beginning with the new birth or being born again, which leads to being "spiritually minded" (Romans 8:5–8; Ephesians 2:2–4; 4:22–24).

When there's mutual respect based on each of us having the faith of Jesus Christ, we can respect and inspire each other to rise in our individual strengths. Mutual respect in Christ encourages an environment where we lovingly submit to each other.

Respect of Persons

Ephesians 5:21:
Submitting yourselves one to another [that's mutually] in the fear [respect] of God [the Greek text reads Christ].

We learned in Chapters 1 through 3 that lording over God's people is not God's will. We saw that Jesus Christ, the Apostle Paul, and the Apostle Peter all stated the same thing: Do not lord over God's people. If this approach of lording over God's people continues unchallenged, it breeds and eventually institutionalizes a "respect of persons" environment.

A respect of persons, a negative concept in the Bible, is when people judge the value of others by natural knowledge (what one can analyze by the senses), and it is rife with bias. These are habits built over years. However, the value of others should be assessed by spiritual knowledge (the revealed Word of God).

Respect of persons eventually promotes an environment where fear can flourish. And it promotes favoritism. Respect of persons produces spiritual blindness and an environment of seeking the favor of others. It isolates and controls through fear. And it breaks unity. Respect of persons is the opposite of mutual respect in Christ.

Deuteronomy 1:17:
Ye shall not respect persons in judgment; *but* ye shall hear the small as well as the great; ye shall not be afraid of the face of

man; for the judgment *is* God's: and the cause that is too hard for you, bring *it* unto me, and I will hear it.

Respect of persons is to be partial to one over another. This applies to everyone. When we think of ourselves as being above OR below others, we are not acknowledging the equality we have in Christ. This is frustrating the grace of God. Verse 17 says, "the small as well as the great." God addresses this value scale in terms of man's viewpoint. Man puts people in categories of comparison like "small and great." These are the natural-knowledge or five-senses judgments according to the flesh that tempt us to "be afraid of the face of man." We are led to believe someone is greater than ourselves or we are greater than others. Both are wrong. That is result of a respect-of-persons environment.

Deuteronomy 16:19:

Thou shalt not wrest judgment [shall not pervert justice, in ESV]; thou shalt not respect persons, neither take a gift: for a gift doth blind the eyes of the wise, and pervert the words of the righteous.

Here in verse 19 "a gift" refers to a bribe. Bribes can come in different forms: financial, emotional, and even moral. Someone who receives a bribe becomes beholden to someone else. They feel they owe something to the person who gave them the bribe.

Guilt is a formidable force with enough energy to carve deep paths in the mind and drive people to do things they would not otherwise do. As a result, some follow these paths loyally without question . . . for years . . .because of guilt. Once someone enters this vicious cycle of obligation, without the light of the Word and humility, they often continue a lifetime of moving back and forth ambivalently, trying to please men instead of God.

How can this happen among believers? The Word tells us "…for a gift doth blind the eyes of the wise." "Eyes" can be a figurative reference to "mental and spiritual faculties," as it is here in Deuteronomy 16:19. People get tricked spiritually so that they no longer "see" clearly what is happening after they take a bribe.

This explains why people at times cannot see their own fruit. Because they say one thing and do another. People can be blinded to the fact that their own words and actions do not line up, even when their hypocrisy is so clearly evident to others. Such are they who have been corrupted by bribes. This is true politically, in business, entertainment, in the media, in academia, as well as in the Christian community. This is the fruit, or result, of being a respecter of persons.

This verse also says, "and pervert the words of the righteous." To "pervert" means to twist or overturn the words of the righteous. When a bribe is involved, the Word of God becomes twisted or overturned in the lives of those who are led captive by the bribe. Then their actions contradict the Word, and it leads to hypocrisy and lying. Where once someone lived with integrity before God and man, there is perversion of the word of the righteous. This is not what we want in the work of the Christian ministry.

When Peter brought the Word to the Gentiles, God showed him a clear revelation. Peter was not to call anything common or unclean that God had cleansed. When Peter went to Cornelius' house, he made a profound statement, "Of a truth I perceive that God is no respecter of persons." (Acts 10:34) That means God does not judge the value of people by man's natural knowledge or five-senses perspective. This lesson is underscored by the fact that Cornelius was a Roman soldier and a Gentile, both detested and shunned by most Judeans of that day.

God started the believers on the right foot at the inception of what we call Christianity. In the Book of Acts, obedience to the household of faith is how they lived the Word in practice. Mutual respect was at the core of their relationships one with another. If Christian believers start with what God did in Christ for each believer, then mutual respect becomes the basis to begin a true biblical relationship. Obedience to the household of faith begins with mutual respect.

Departing From the Faith

I Timothy 4:1–2:

Now the Spirit [God] speaketh expressly, that in the latter times some shall depart from the faith [the household faith], giving heed to seducing spirits, and doctrines of devils;

Speaking lies in hypocrisy; having their conscience seared with a hot iron.

In recent years, much attention has been paid to this topic regarding "some shall depart from the faith." First, we must remember that the household of faith is not about grouping ourselves in a location or branding ourselves with a name. The household of faith is spiritual and is accessible only through grace. It is framed by truth regarding Jesus Christ. No one has the ability, right, or authority to excommunicate, remove, or cut off someone else from the household of faith. Individuals decide to depart by their own choice and character. God placed each one of His children in His family. God's decision stands.

John 10:29

My Father, which gave *them* me, is greater than all; and no *man* is able to pluck *them* out of my Father's hand.

Because the household of faith has no location, organization, or affiliation, it may be difficult to understand based on natural knowledge. People must believe in what they cannot physically see. The Word of

God is what provides the structure for the household of faith. We stand within the boundaries of truth regarding the common faith of Jesus Christ that we all share as brothers and sisters in the family of God.

Therefore, when someone who is instructed in the household of faith chooses to depart from it, their departure is not contingent upon location or group affiliation. Their departure takes place in the heart. They withdraw from the truth of God's Word that frames the household of faith. They depart from divine grace to their own works in attempt to be accepted by God. And when someone departs from the household of faith it eventually becomes noticeable in decisions, words, actions, and practical errors, culminating in doctrinal error.

I Corinthians 12:25:

That there should be no schism in the body; but *that* the members should have the same care one for another.

Care one for another is a characteristic of unified Christians. We are not to judge by natural knowledge; instead, we value each other in Christ. We do not love anyone less than another, nor do we ignore people or slight people. We are to have the same care one for another. So, if someone chooses to depart from the household of faith (this assumes that at some point they have been instructed and embraced the household of faith), they will likely become a respecter of persons by judging the value of others according to natural knowledge and not according to Christ in them. They will ignore the Christ in each of us, which is that treasure in earthen vessels (II Corinthians 4:5–7). To depart from the faith is to depart from its basic practical component of mutual respect, which is rooted in the accomplished work of Jesus Christ applied to all of us.

If we have fallen into the error of being a respecter of persons, we must be honest before God to correct our thinking, because it is spiritually wrong and produces fear. It makes people susceptible to blinding bribes and it perverts the words of the righteous.

The Book of II Timothy is the last known written communication of God's Word by the Apostle Paul. It was under Paul's ministry that it was recorded, "So mightily grew the word of God and prevailed" (Acts 19:20). This spectacular outreach occurred in the Asia Minor area. The best we know, the first-century church began its decline after this point.

Paul sadly noted in II Timothy 1:15 that ". . . all they which are in Asia be turned away from me." This began a downward spiral regarding the truth about Jesus Christ. Because people missed the mark regarding the truth (II Timothy 2:18), it was followed by resisting or opposing "the truth" (II Timothy 3:8) and concluded with turning "away *their* ears from the truth . . . unto fables." (II Timothy 4:4) Christianity has contended with fables in place of truth ever since.

The word "from" in II Timothy 4:4 is a preposition meaning "away from" the "exterior" or surface of something. The truth had not actually penetrated their hearts, their interior, but was only given a surface consideration. This condition exists when the truth no longer reaches the heart of a person. It is as if they cannot even hear the truth. It only reaches the surface. So instead of really hearing and turning to truth, they turn to fables.

The word "fables" in this verse is the Greek word *muthos*, and it means "anything delivered by word of mouth." It can be contrasted with truth. These fables are myths—things people imagine and make up. Even when people who are considered authorities avow to the veracity of such fables, they are still in fact not true. These fables or myths do not refer to "it is written." Rather they refer to anything delivered person-to-person by word of mouth.

It is striking to note in current times the level of consideration often given to such word of mouth "fables" which are no more than opinions, preferences, and agenda-driven edicts of men. If one bothers to earnestly dissect them, typically the discovery is they contain infinitesimal amounts of truth, or no truth at all! Yet, they are treated as if God Himself has delivered them. The fruit of such fables is bondage, in some form, as opposed to the truth which is freedom.

Remember Acts 21:23 when they rejected what Paul had to say about the wonderful things God was doing? Paul was speaking truth. They responded, "Do therefore this that we say to thee." This is how myths work: People speak their edicts, opinions, rules, and commandments of men as opposed to speaking truth. And eventually these fables replace the truth.

"Fables" is in the plural form in II Timothy 4:4, so it is multiple myths. Once one myth circulates and is accepted, there will be more that follow, building on the first one.

For example, it is a myth to believe that any Christian group or ministry is the same as the household of faith. It is not a biblically sound doctrine. It is a myth to think one denomination, sect, or group exclusively represents Christianity. Consequently, another myth follows saying that individuals who leave or are ejected from such a Christian group are departing from the household of faith. One must begin with the premise that their group is exclusively divine. Such assertions cut at the heart of the faith of Jesus Christ we all share as brothers and sisters in God's family and lead to confusion and hurt.

Once I was visiting with a fellow minister while waiting for a printing project. We had an enthusiastic conversation about the Word of God. Then he asked me, "What church are you with?" He meant what denomination was I representing. I looked at him and said, "You of all people know there is only one church." He looked at me with an expression as if he had suddenly awakened out of sleep and must orient himself. After a brief reflection, he smiled with a twinkle in his eye and said, "You are right!" At that moment, manmade denominational boundaries were dissolved. We both knew I was speaking of the Body of Christ.

Myths can quickly lead to false accusations and do not represent the truth. The harm caused by such baseless rhetoric is immeasurable. These myths, if not refuted, become mental penitentiaries that incarcerate people. To refute each myth, people must have and experience truth to be made free (John 8:31–32). Myths eventually develop into doctrines of men.

Matthew 15:9, 12-14:

But in vain they [the Pharisees that Jesus called hypocrites] do worship me, teaching *for* doctrines the commandments of men.

Then came his disciples, and said unto him, Knowest thou that the Pharisees were offended, after they heard this saying?

But he answered and said, Every plant, which my heavenly Father hath not planted, shall be rooted up.

Let them alone: they be blind leaders of the blind. And if the blind lead the blind, both shall fall into the ditch.

Myths are men's ideas and are like weeds that grow in the garden of people's minds and choke out truth. Whenever myths take root, the result will always be the commandments of men taught as doctrine. God did not plant such ideas, men did.

What allows these myths to take root is an environment of respect of persons. We may have heard something like, "Because so and so said it, it must be true!" People revere the words of men above the Word of God without checking the veracity of what is stated and whether it lines up according to the Scriptures.

Acts 17:11:

These [Judeans of Berea] were more noble than those in Thessalonica, in that they received the word with all readiness of mind, and searched the scriptures daily, whether those things were so.

The Judeans of Berea received the Word from the Apostle Paul, yet they had the right heart to go to the Scriptures they had access to and see the truth for themselves. This is a great practice for all Christian believers. This practice really helps to keep respect of persons at bay.

Myths become commandments of men and are then taught for doctrine. As you recall, doctrine is right teaching or the standard for how to conduct our life. In other words, myths become the standard of whether something is right or wrong. As already mentioned, when you have one myth, more myths will follow, and that is why it's in the plural form. It is the same with the "doctrines [plural] and commandments [plural] of men." (Mark 7:7) With each myth comes more erosion of truth. This is how denominationalism and disagreements develop among Christian groups today. Schisms represent the splintered factions of the church that began on Pentecost. A root cause of the schisms is myths.

There is an extremely healthy element to having different Christian groups that spread the gospel throughout the world (Acts 1:8, 8:4; Romans 1:5, 16:26). Such activity protects against the adversary working through men to achieve one universal Christian organization that can lord over God's people more easily.[21] Smaller groups provide more access to interact on a personal level. This interaction allows for mutual care for each other and more accountability on the Scripture.

---

21   An example of such a universal Christian organization was the Church of England from which some 20,000 Puritans, predominantly families, fled from its tyranny and religious persecution to the new world in the early 1600s with the intent to establish religious freedom for themselves and their posterity. See endnote for David McCullough.

This is like what the Lord Jesus Christ taught on the night he was betrayed, "If I then, *your* Lord and Master, have washed your feet; ye also ought to wash one another's feet." (John 13:14)

Washing each other's feet indicated the humility to perform tasks as a servant to one another. Such hospitality demonstrated care one for another. Jesus clearly set this as an example for his followers. Especially noteworthy is the fact that this act was performed on the night when he was under tremendous pressure, knowing of his impending suffering. Amazing! Mutual care one for another is a great truth for all believers to learn.

The result of lording over God's people is an environment that silently or openly endorses respect of persons instead of genuine respect based on having the same faith of Jesus Christ. Whenever myths take root, a respect-of-persons environment is taking root. This is when courageous men, women, and young people must speak up to bring the focus back to Jesus Christ and all that he accomplished for us. As Edmund Burke, an eighteenth-century Irish statesman, said, "All that is necessary for the triumph of evil is that good men do nothing."[22]

II Timothy 4:1–2:

I charge *thee* therefore before God, and the Lord Jesus Christ, who shall judge the quick and the dead at his appearing and his kingdom;

Preach the word; be instant in season, out of season [when it's convenient and when it's not convenient]; reprove, rebuke, exhort with all longsuffering ["Longsuffering is that quality of

---

22 Burke further developed this idea by stating, "Whilst men are linked together, they easily and speedily communicate the alarm of any evil design. They are enabled to fathom it with common counsel, and to oppose it with united strength . . . When bad men combine, the good must associate; else they will fall, one by one, an unpitied sacrifice in a contemptible struggle." See endnote for Edmund Burke.

self-restraint in the face of provocation which does not hastily retaliate or promptly punish; it is the opposite of anger, and is associated with mercy, and is used of God, Ex.34:6 (Sept.)"] and doctrine.

It takes teaching, patience, and being ". . . swift to hear, slow to speak, slow to wrath . . ." (James 1:19) to bring people back to what is right according to the Word—the true doctrine. There will need to be reproof—pointing out what is wrong and redirecting to what is right. To reset the right standard of the grace of God and the faith of Jesus Christ takes encouragement. God will never leave us alone throughout this whole process. We can begin by getting quiet on the inside, recognizing His presence, and acknowledging the truth.

Psalm 46:10:

Be still, and know that I am God . . .

"Be still and know that I am God." The first thing to ensure that we are personally understanding the Word is to get with God and be still with Him. God is the God of mercy, which every one of us needs! For those who have been in an environment where respect of persons existed, there may need to be a release of mental weights. Tightly clenching our fists around guilt, anger, bitterness, and resentment must be replaced by an open hand that receives the healing power of forgiveness. We must approach our task in love and not have any remnant of bitterness, anger, or ill will toward anyone.

Ephesians 4:31–32:

Let all bitterness, and wrath, and anger, and clamour, and evil speaking, be put away from you, with all malice [ill will, desire to injure]:

And be ye kind one to another, tenderhearted, forgiving one another, even as God for Christ's sake hath forgiven you.

Forgiveness is not a compromise on the Word—it is the Word! Forgiveness is a necessary ingredient in all healing of the body and mind. The adversary of God's people, Satan, will endeavor to hinder, obstruct, and even pursue you in this struggle. Why? Because you are endeavoring to restore the Word in yourself and others. Remember Ephesians 6:12 says, "For we wrestle not against flesh and blood."

Jesus Christ brought up this struggle and spiritual fight on the night he was betrayed as he worked with Peter on an individual basis.

Luke 22:31:

And the Lord said, Simon, Simon, behold, Satan hath desired [to demand for oneself] to have *you*, that he may sift you as wheat.

This is what our spiritual adversary wants. He is the real enemy. He wants to sift us as wheat. The wheat refers to the valuable part of the grain, as opposed to the chaff, which was considered without worth and thrown out. This is a figure of speech, a simile, which means that Satan wants the most valuable part of our lives—our skills, our time, our loyalty of heart, our strengths, and abilities—in order to waste them on spiritually fruitless endeavors.

This is part of how Satan resists the true God, by keeping truth from becoming known. He occupies and distracts God's people with endeavors that exhaust their strengths and resources. When this occurs, the believers' strengths and resources have been wasted. They are flushed away into the gutters of fruitless endeavors. On the surface, they may appear to have value, but eventually the fruit will show itself. We must decide Satan cannot have them; they belong to God to benefit His purposes and His people!

Luke 22:32:
> But I have prayed for thee, that thy [the] faith [Peter believing God] fail not: and when thou art converted, strengthen thy brethren.

After Peter made that transition, the next thing he was to do was to strengthen the brethren. And that is exactly what we need to do. As believers and leaders in the church, we should never allow ourselves to surrender our integrity on the Word and become respecters of persons with the fear, the bribery, and the blindness that follow.

Fear and intimidation are not good counselors. A searching soul never grasps what to do next in life out of fear or intimidation. First remove the fear or intimidation, and then what to do will become clearer. You get rid of fear by acting on the Word.

Proverbs 19:21:
> *There are* many devices in a man's heart; nevertheless the counsel of the Lord, that shall stand.

Let God be our counselor. We can read His Word and understand what He wants. Service and the work of the Christian ministry—whether by the individual or in shared service—should be Word-centered only. This will produce the good works in love that spring forth from the grace of God living in our souls.

So how do we keep the Word first in our service? It is by being obedient to the household faith. Obedience begins with maintaining that genuine respect in Christ for others in God's family, which must begin with respect for ourselves. Our identity in Christ should be treasured in each of us. As we each recognize these truths, believe, and embrace them as God's Word, we can then help others. We tenderly and lovingly reach out to our brothers and sisters, strengthening them as we share and teach them these truths in love.

At the end of Paul's life, he wrote these words in II Timothy 4:7: "I have fought a good fight, I have finished my course, I have kept the faith." He did not say he kept the ministry or even the Body of Christ— he said he kept the faith. That is the faith of Jesus Christ that we all share in, the household faith, God's family. To keep the faith is to obey the faith. Paul, of all people, knew that obedience to the household of faith is the practical foundation upon which the truth of the Body of Christ is lived. The household of faith emphasizes who we are as sons of God—our identity in Christ. The Body of Christ is more about the service we perform interdependently based on that identity—our potential in Christ.

Obedience to the faith begins with mutual respect based on the accomplished work of Christ. Our response to the Christian dilemma is simple: move ahead with grace and keep the faith. This is part of the one-accord response needed in our day and time. It is time to act and reach out and preach this Word, the very truth that will make people free!

Chapter 5

OBEDIENCE TO THE HOUSEHOLD OF FAITH

O bedience to the household of faith is built upon obeying God rather than men. The foundation of obeying God is submitting to His accomplished work in Christ for us and in us. Grace is the unmerited divine favor by which we were offered the work and the sacrifice of Jesus Christ as though they are our own. This is our identity in Christ.

Although this accomplished work is offered to us freely, we must still choose it over obedience to men. Obeying men is to submit to the work and will of men, including our own accomplishments, even though God is offering His grace. There is nothing wrong with accomplishing things in life and enjoying them, but for the Christian what we do or accomplish is not the basis of who we are. Our identity—and therefore our purpose, meaning, and strength of living—is drawn from one or the other, grace or works. The desire to accomplish earthly and temporal works according to the rules of the world *as an identity* is at odds with the eternal and heavenly identity given to us through Christ. The former fades over time, the latter lasts into eternity.

Despite these competing forces, grace is able to successfully guide believers into their new calling in Christ as sons of God, eternal and seated in heaven. (Ephesians 2:6) Works push and intimidate in the opposite direction to get us to identify with the accomplishments of men (including our own), which are earthly and temporal.

Understanding grace requires humility to God and His revealed Word. It glorifies God and testifies to His boundless love. Grace can only be understood spiritually. It is beyond senses man to identify with a God who sees His children only through the work of His only begotten son.

On the other hand, the world demands worldly accomplishments that are judged according to the standards of man and will ultimately glorify men. These works are understood by natural knowledge. Obedience to the faith is the demonstration to elevate grace above works in terms of defining who we are as Christians. Though this obedience is an individual decision, it inherently remains a family endeavor we do together. Helping one another in God's family is a necessary component of this obedience.

In the beginning of the Christian church as recorded in Acts 2, followers met with little resistance. The fledgling church enjoyed a brief time before Satan, the supposed god of this world or age (II Corinthians 4:4), marshaled opposition. Ironically, resistance came from religious leaders, who should have been supportive. They were men of social position cloaked in *religious* garb. They opposed and directly commanded the apostles to not take up the cause of Christ. This set up the same type of dichotomy we see today, with so-called spiritual leaders choosing to obey men rather than God. This struggle is at the heart of the Christian leadership dilemma.

Acts 5:28–29:

Saying, Did not we straitly command you that ye should not teach in this name [the name of Jesus Christ]? and, behold, ye have filled Jerusalem with your doctrine, and intend to bring this man's blood upon us.

Then Peter and the *other* apostles answered and said, We ought to obey God rather than men.

Obeying God rather than men is at the crux of obedience to the household of faith and is the path that resolves the Christian leadership dilemma. The word "obey" here means "obey one in authority." That one in authority is God. A demonstration of this obedience to God is to speak boldly for Him, as the apostles were doing when they were challenged.

Acts 5:30–32:

The God of our fathers raised up Jesus, whom ye slew and hanged on a tree.

Him hath God exalted with his right hand *to be* a Prince and a Saviour, for to give repentance to Israel, and forgiveness of sins.

And we are his witnesses of these things; and *so is* also the Holy Ghost [the gift as evidenced by one who has taken ownership to use it], whom God hath given to them that obey him.

"Obey" in verse 32 is the same word as in verse 29. Peter and the apostles were witnesses attesting to the truth regarding the crucifixion and resurrection of Jesus Christ. Later they witnessed his ascension into heaven, where he is now seated at God's right hand. Soon after that, they received God's gift of holy spirit, which itself is a witness of these truths.

Jesus prophesied that the apostles by way of the gift of holy spirit would be a witness unto the ends of the earth.

Acts 1:8:

But ye shall receive [Greek *lambanō*–take ownership to use] power, after that the Holy Ghost is come upon you: and ye shall be witnesses unto me both in Jerusalem, and in all Judaea, and in Samaria, and unto the uttermost part of the earth.

Prior to Jesus Christ's ascension into heaven, he left the apostles with specific instructions to take ownership of and use the gift of holy spirit with its inherent power. For all intents and purposes, the Christian experience is still launched today from this same foundation. This personal ownership and utilization of the gift of holy spirit are what elevate the Christian believer to be a witness for God. Logically then, obeying God involves taking ownership of and using the power that Christ said would be offered. With Christ's endorsement of this power, we can have confidence in the faith of Jesus Christ, which entitles us to salvation and the ability to walk like Christ.

Jude 1:20:

But ye, beloved, building up yourselves on your most holy faith [the faith of Jesus Christ, according to Romans 3:22; Galatians 2:16], praying in the Holy Ghost [the gift of holy spirit].

Praying in the holy spirit refers to speaking in tongues.[23] Speaking in tongues can be used for perfect prayer (in private) and to speak a

---

23 Speaking in tongues is one way the spirit is evidenced or manifested, I Corinthians 12:7–10. Speaking in tongues is a Spirit (God) to spirit (gift) language of men or angels, always unknown to the speaker, used primarily for

message to others (in public) when interpreted. By praying perfectly in the spirit, believers build confidence upon the accomplished work of Christ, which can be expressed as the faith of Jesus Christ.

It is this faith of Jesus Christ that is common to all of God's children (Titus 1:4), hence the household faith (Galatians 6:10). The word "faith," as noted in I Corinthians 12:9, is the faith of Jesus Christ, which is what God energizes within the believer to carry out the works of Christ and greater works (John 14:12). The greater works are that believers can act in concert one with another as equal sons of God in the Body of Christ—something Christ could not do.

When the apostles taught and did the works of Christ in his name, it caused intense jealousy among the religious leaders, who then demanded they obey men rather than God.

Acts 5:15–17:

Insomuch that they brought forth the sick into the streets, and laid *them* on beds and couches, that at the least the shadow of Peter passing by might overshadow some of them.

There came also a multitude *out* of the cities round about unto Jerusalem, bringing sick folks, and them which were vexed with unclean spirits: and they were healed everyone.

Then the high priest rose up, and all they that were with him, (which is the sect of the Sadducees,) and were filled with indignation [jealousy].

The apostles were carrying out the works of Christ—in healing people from physical maladies as well as evil spirit control. Obeying God by taking ownership and using the gift of the holy spirit is part of how Christian believers can practically work together in concert with other

---

personal prayer that builds on the foundation of faith, and is on occasion a public sign from God that is to be interpreted.

brothers and sisters according to the faith. Yet, some of the religious leaders of that day became jealous and did not approve of this activity.

Acts 5:33:

> When they heard *that*, they were cut *to the heart*, and took counsel to slay them.

The words "they were cut" are translated from a Greek verb meaning "to saw asunder or in twain [two], to divide by a saw." They were not literally divided, but figuratively they were "sawn through mentally." They were continuously being cut on the inside by the words spoken by Peter and the other apostles. These antagonists erupted at the declaration of the apostles who boldly spoke the Word. Only the Word of God has the power and precision to make such a separation.

Hebrews 4:12:

> For the word of God *is* quick, and powerful, and sharper than any twoedged sword, piercing even to the dividing asunder of soul and spirit, and of the joints and marrow, and is a discerner of the thoughts and intents of the heart.

Obedience to Others Has Its Place

There's nothing wrong with voluntary obedience to others. Students are to obey their teachers, employees are to obey their employers (Ephesians 6:5), and so on. Most civilized societies have these social norms, and it is encouraged by God (I Peter 2:13–17). Spiritually, in truth, there is everything *right* with it.

- In Romans 13:1, it states we are to be subject to the higher powers (the context is ministers who serve in the church of the Body of Christ).

- It also says in Ephesians 5:21 that we are to submit ourselves one to another in the respect of God (the Greek text reads "Christ").
- This is how God instructs children to conduct themselves ". . . obey your parents in the Lord . . ." (Ephesians 6:1). This obedience sets the pattern for young minds and hearts to develop as they learn about their identity, maturity, and stand in Christ.

So, there is no problem with voluntary obedience to others in the proper context that does not contradict God's Word.

Christian leaders, as well as every believer in the church, have strengths to share in specific areas where they are most spiritually adept to perform. In the balanced Christian walk, each of us follows and leads depending on the need at the time. The key is allowing love to motivate us and sound biblical wisdom to guide our endeavors.

Obedience to the Household Faith

Romans 1:5:

By whom we have received grace and apostleship, for obedience [*hupakoē* obedience, as the result of attentive hearing a noun form of the verb *hupakouō*] to the [household] faith among all nations, for his name.

In the Book of Romans, the foundational treatise to the Christian church, we see that spiritual instruction begins with obedience to the household of faith. This obedience can and should be lived among all nations of the earth. This foundation for the Christian community cannot be overstated. This obedience is a result of attentive hearing. It comes from a Greek verb transliterated *hupakouō* (it occurs here in its noun form *hupakoē*). This Greek verb means "to hear" and carries a sense of "stillness or attention in order to answer."

Let's see this concept of obedience, which is hearing to the end of obeying, from the Book of Acts.

Hearing to the End of Obeying

In Acts 12, Peter was arrested and put into prison by King Herod. The believers prayed for Peter, and God intervened via an angel and released Peter from prison. He then went to the house where believers were praying.

Acts 12:12–13:

And when he had considered *the thing* [Peter considering his astonishing release from prison by an angel], he came to the house of Mary the mother of John, whose surname was Mark; where many were gathered together praying.

And as Peter knocked at the door of the gate, a damsel came to hearken, named Rhoda.

Rhoda heard Peter's knock and she came to open the door. The word "hearken" is translated from *hupakouō*. She heard, she paid attention, and she responded with action. This is a remarkably simple illustration to understand the meaning of the word "obedience."

The example of Rhoda is literal, yet this understanding can be applied to the spiritual walk. Hearing God can be a delicate experience at times and requires stillness and attentiveness as God gets our attention and moves in us. Developing good habits of listening is important. What we listen to and who we listen to does determine a lot of our success in life. Eliminating or at least reducing the intake of the endless din and onslaught of negativity around us that yields no good fruit in our life is wisdom because words matter. We should surround ourselves with counsel from loving and sound thinking people.

It is paramount that God gets first place in our hearts that we may hear Him above anyone or anything else. At times this requires removing from our daily routines the distractions that hinder a peaceful and attentive state in which we can recognize God's gentle movements in our hearts.

Psalms 46:10:

Be still, [to cease from labor; to be unoccupied; to have time or opportunity for] and know [experientially] that I *am* God: I will be exalted among the heathen, I will be exalted in the earth.

The phrase "Be still and know that I am God" carries a sense of expectation, as if one is deliberately holding their own labor or effort in reserve, to be unoccupied with other matters to have time and undivided attention to God. This devoted action allows believers to experience His power and sovereignty above man and nature. When God is knocking on the door of our hearts, we want to be unoccupied and have time or opportunity to respond accordingly. We listen for the "still small voice" (I Kings 19:12)[24] as He moves in us and with us.

When obedience is applied to the household of faith, Christians should insist that only God's judgment be entertained in our hearts. When and where the judgments of men contradict God, such judgments of men should be discarded. This is especially important when it comes to obeying God rather than men. To obey the household of faith is to obey God's judicial decision to acquit man of sin and guilt and make man acceptable to Him. This legal decision was accomplished

---

24 "... the sound of a low whisper," English Standard Version of the Bible.

on our behalf through the sacrifice of Christ. Christ is the answer that supersedes man's continuous attempts to produce perfection on earth, whether that perfection be personal or societal. Perfection is found in the accomplished work of Christ.

Adam's Disobedience

God's justice requires a legal substitute to pay for Adam's disobedience. Adam was the first man and the consequences of Adam's actions passed on to all men. And these consequences are severe. As a result, man's heritage through Adam—what man receives at birth—is sin nature. The sin nature produces the collective habits of disobedience to God developed by each person. These habits become each person's "old man."[25]

That is one reason why children are instructed to "obey their parents in the Lord" (Ephesians 6:1), to curtail the development of these habits of disobedience. These habits reside in everyone, to varying degrees, yet they can be kept in check through raising children "in the nurture and admonition of the Lord" (Ephesians 6:4). For the born-again Christian, the old man is crucified with Christ (Romans 6:6), but the old man behavior remains an option for the Christian to serve and obey.

Parents represent God to their children as the most significant points of contact in their young lives. Because young children do not understand or know God, obedience to parents is the first step in learning obedience to God. This prepares them for when they reach an age of spiritual accountability. The parents' responsibility is to remain "in the Lord" (Ephesians 6:1), which means they retain the master (Christ) servant (believer) relationship in their own walks in newness of life according to the Word.

---

25   Romans 6:6; Ephesians 4:22; Colossians 3:9.

This sin nature develops habits of disobedience to God in each person uniquely based on upbringing, exposure to the Word and godly principles, and free will. This sin nature is the origin of these habits, but in the believer the "old man" has been crucified with Christ. At the conclusion of man's time on earth, man receives an inheritance from Adam, which is death (with only one exception).[26]

Romans 5:12 and 19:
Wherefore, as by one man [Adam] sin entered into the world, and death by sin; and so death passed upon all men, for that all have sinned.

For as by one man's [Adam] disobedience many were made sinners, so by the obedience of one [Jesus Christ] shall many be made righteous.

There is only one substitute accepted by God to pay the price for the consequences of sin and death passed on from Adam. It is the sacrifice of Jesus Christ who "became obedient unto . . . the death of the cross." (Philippians 2:8) This is generally understood as the fundamental bedrock of Christianity. For the Christian believer, the "old man" is crucified with Christ (Romans 6:6). And then comes the opportunity of living a new lifestyle in Christ (Romans 6:4). Such a lifestyle, walking in "newness of life," still requires freewill decisions.

Justified by the Faith of Jesus Christ

In the sight of God as the supreme judge, nothing man does can achieve justification (legally made right) before God. Only the faith

---

26   The only exception to all men dying is the Christian believer who is alive at the time of Christ's return. These people will not die but be changed, the mortal will be made immortal, I Thessalonians 4:13–18; I Corinthians 15:51–58.

of Jesus Christ, his entire perfect life and sacrifice, is an acceptable substitute.

Romans 1:16–17:

For I am not ashamed of the gospel of [that pertains to] Christ: for it is the power of God unto salvation to everyone that believeth; to the Jew [Judean] first, and also to the Greek [Gentile].

For therein is the righteousness of God revealed from faith [believe God raised the Lord Jesus from the dead[27]] to faith [the faith of Jesus Christ]: as it is written, The just shall live [or may be translated as "keep on living" indicating an ongoing progressive future] by [out of] faith [of Jesus Christ].

The just or righteous will continue to live in the present and eventually eternally. The righteous will not merely exist on earth in the present but truly live in all the beauty and wonder it is to be God's children in His design from the soil to the heavens. Nature as man's home and classroom is open for enjoyment, stewardship, utilization, and learning. And the righteous will live as eternal beings initiated at the return of Christ. This is the depth of these verses and what the faith of Jesus Christ has opened to mankind.

The Judean and the Gentile are natural men of body and soul, and as natural men they can believe God. From believing God raised the Lord Jesus from the dead to the faith of Jesus Christ is how salvation is provided. The natural man does not have the faith of Jesus Christ, but natural man can believe God. And when a natural man (or woman)

---

27 Romans 10:9 and 10: That if thou shalt confess with thy mouth the Lord Jesus, and shalt believe in thine heart that God hath raised him from the dead, thou shalt be saved. For with the heart man believeth unto righteousness; and with the mouth confession is made unto salvation.

confesses with their mouth the Lord Jesus and believes in their heart that God raised him from the dead, they are saved (Romans 10:9–10). By believing this truth, each person receives the faith of Jesus Christ. After that point, the Christian no longer relies on their own believing but on the faith of Christ.

So, faith is provided by God, and believing God is what man must do to receive it. The faith of Jesus Christ represents his believing God to the uttermost. He accomplished God's plan of redemption for man. This is at the very foundation of obedience to the household of faith.

Galatians 2:16:

Knowing that a man is not justified by the works of the law, but by the faith of Jesus Christ, even we have believed in Jesus Christ, that we might be justified by the faith of Christ, and not by the works of the law: for by the works of the law shall no flesh be justified.

That is so clear! Justification is the legal decision by God to acquit man of guilt and sin and to declare man acceptable to Him. God is the final judge, and He is the one who justifies man. It was His legal decision to acquit man of guilt and sin. What gets man across the *finish line* in the pursuit of eternal life is the faith of Jesus Christ.

The believing action that Jesus took concluded when he uttered these words on the cross moments before he died, "It is finished." (John 19:30) It was his believing God to complete his work as man's redeemer that God bundled and gave to mankind as the faith of Jesus Christ. To Jesus, it was believing God to the end; to us, as a completed work, it is the faith of Jesus Christ. Why? Because Jesus Christ is no longer believing to achieve our rescue. The work of Christ accomplished our substitution. It is finished, we are complete in Christ, lacking nothing (Colossians 2:10).

Galatians 3:22:

But the scripture hath concluded all under sin, that the promise by faith of Jesus Christ might be given to them that believe.

In Romans 1:17, "from faith to faith" means anyone who desires, believes God by accepting the sacrifice of Christ receives the faith of Christ. The faith of Christ bridges the gulf between unsaved man and God. It is only through his faith that the impossible is made possible. A natural man with the sentence of death confesses Christ and believes that God raised him from the dead, and then he becomes justified as a spiritual man with eternal life abiding within him.

Galatians 3:23:

But before faith [of Jesus Christ] came, we were kept under the law, shut up unto the faith [of Jesus Christ] which should afterwards be revealed.

Jesus Christ had to fulfill the Law and so "the faith of Jesus Christ" came after this was completed. Only then could his work of believing God be applied to mankind as "faith." To those of us who live after Pentecost, his believing was revealed as faith, because he is no longer believing God to achieve our redemption. It has been done—it is finished! It is as if God packaged Jesus' believing and gave it to us as the faith or belief of Jesus Christ. To believe and act on this truth is the essence of our identity in Christ.

The faith of Jesus Christ is common to all born-again believers. God is our Father, we are His children, and that is why it's a family—the household faith. This is tremendous because Christians who apply these truths can live a higher quality of life, not as victims, but as being spiritually successful as true victors in the struggles of life. A more-than-conqueror mindset is built on our justification (legally made right with God) through the faith of Jesus Christ.

The Supreme Judge

When men judge in place of God, it opens the door for all kinds of hurtful and false accusations, judgments, condemnations, and criticisms. When Christians submit to the judgment of men, in matters in which God is solely responsible, people suffer unnecessarily. People then go on to seek approval, acceptance, and permission from each other when God has already given them approval, acceptance, and permission to live free in Christ.

God's endorsement is based on our justification in Jesus Christ because we have been acquitted of all guilt and sin. We are now and forever acceptable to God. It is only when Christians are obedient to the household of faith that the judgments of men are refused, and God's judgment alone stands and matters to them.

I Corinthians 4:1–3:

Let a man so account of us, as of the ministers of Christ, and stewards of the mysteries of God.

Moreover it is required in stewards, that a man be found faithful.

But with me it is a very small thing that I should be judged of you, or of man's judgment:[28] yea, I judge not mine own self.

Paul rejected three categories of judgment found in verse 3. All three judgments are grown in the petri dish of natural or worldly knowledge. The first category he noted was the "carnal Christians." Paul wrote, "It is a very small thing that I should be judged of you." He was talking to

---

28 The English Standard Version of the Bible translates the phrase "of man's judgment" as "by any human court."

the Corinthian believers who were dominated by a carnal perspective (spiritual children by the new birth yet dominated by natural knowledge). By revelation from God, Paul wrote two letters (epistles) specifically showing where they had missed the mark. He reminded them, among other things, of the foundational truth of justification found in Romans.

One clear example of the Corinthians' tendency toward natural knowledge is in Chapter 3. The Corinthians were elevating natural knowledge in finding their identity in Paul or Apollos, both ministers, when it should have been in Christ. The accomplished work of Christ is the only proper foundation upon which to build a Christian life.

I Corinthians 3:4 and 11:

For while one saith, I am of Paul; and another, I *am* of Apollos; are ye not carnal?

For other foundation can no man lay than that is laid, which is Jesus Christ.

The second category in I Corinthians 4:3 is "man's judgment." The word "judgment" is "day," so it can be understood as *man's day*. This is referring to the world's judgment. In this era of the church of Grace, God allows the judgment of men to "air" (mostly hot air) for a time because the Law of Moses has been fulfilled and no longer is the standard for judgment. Christ is no longer personally present to judge man either.

That is why today we see such vile and degrading judgment and accusations. All around us people are judged by their looks, education, ancestry, socioeconomic background, performance, race, gender, what clothes they wear, and what kind of car they drive. The list goes on *ad infinitum*.

Whenever the judgments of men decrease your value or mine as a child of God, we must obey God rather than men because God states just the opposite. This is not to say we never do anything wrong, and we are not to be called out on such things. The point is simple, even with all our mistakes (and we all make them), our value (i.e., worth) as a son of the living God never decreases in His eyes. When we obey God rather than men, we do not fall prey to such worldly judgments.

The third category in verse 3 of Chapter 4 is "judge not my own self." This may be the most challenging of the three. We are not to even judge ourselves! We submit to the judgment of God, not to carnal Christians, not to the world, and not even to our own selves. That is what it means to obey God rather than men. This is so important when it comes to being obedient to the household of faith.

The phrases in I Corinthians 4:3, "I should be judged" and "I judge" are translated from two Greek words forming one compound word *anakrinō*. These two words translated separately are *ana* "again" and *krinō* "judge." This one Greek word has legal implications and is used forensically of a judge who holds "an investigation; to interrogate, examine, the accused." What Paul is meaning here becomes very clear. Why would we again judge or allow anyone (including ourselves) to conduct an investigation as if they were a judge when God has already judged and ruled in our favor? That is called "double jeopardy."

In the United States, it is unconstitutional to be put in jeopardy, or judged, twice for the same crime after being acquitted. Some trace this concept back to Roman law reflected in the phrase *non bis in idem*, which is Latin for "not twice against the same." God has already justified us through the faith of Jesus Christ. We have already been acquitted of guilt and sin and made acceptable unto Him. Why would we allow another trial to be held when God has already swung the gavel and closed the case? We are free in Christ Jesus.

It is also noted in this context (verses 1 and 2) that we are to be found faithful as stewards. In this context, we can understand part of what faithful means. Here, faithful is to not allow ourselves to be judged again when God has justified us through the faith of Jesus Christ. We should not entertain judgments about ourselves that contradict our God-given justification. To do so is to overrule God. We want to obey God, not men, and this includes not giving in to our own self-judgment!

God's legal decision to acquit man of guilt and sin through Christ and to declare man acceptable is the only appropriate judgment. This is what it means to obey God. To allow self-judgment or condemnation, in which our true value as sons of God is tarnished, is to "crucify . . . the Son of God afresh, and put him to an open shame" (Hebrews 6:6), which is to overrule God.

I Corinthians 4:4:

> For I know nothing by myself; yet am I not hereby justified: but he that judgeth me is the Lord.

The English Standard Version of verse 4 reads: "For I am not aware of anything against myself, but I am not thereby acquitted. It is the Lord who judges me." In essence, Paul wrote, *I'm not even aware of anything that I should judge myself on. I am not using my own awareness of wrongs I have or may have committed as a standard, I am going to let God be the judge.* That's obeying God rather than men.

Without the justification by the faith of Jesus Christ, believers seek justification from other people. That justification then becomes a source of acceptance, approval, and permission from men rather than God. This approach, if unchecked, leads to a respecter-of-persons attitude. People then judge the value of other people by carnal or worldly standards. Consequently, condemnation and all types of biblically unsound judgments follow.

Romans 8:1:

> *There is* therefore now no condemnation to them which are in Christ Jesus . . .

This word "condemnation" means "sentence pronounced against." There is no sentence pronounced against us, now or in the future, because 1 Thessalonians 1:10 and Romans 5:9 tell us we are delivered from the wrath (one possible outcome from judgment) to come.

Worldly judgments, like negatives, tend to stick to us and weigh us down if we are not paying attention. Before we know it, we have a sense of heaviness and being burdened down. Life becomes sluggish and difficult.

This reminds me of the time I once walked through mud and my shoes instantly became caked with mud and noticeably heavier. It became difficult to walk. When I came in the house, I thought I had cleaned off the mud but noticed I left a trail of the mud that still stuck to me. Negatives like bitterness, judgment, and condemnation are just like that. They can stick to us and make our steps heavy. It requires a conscious effort to recognize and remove such influences from our lives.

The Walk of the Flesh and of the Spirit

Obedience to the household of faith also draws the line between the walk of the flesh and the walk by the spirit. The walk by the spirit is to obey God. The walk of the flesh is to obey men. If we are going to obey God, we begin by obeying His Word. Walking by the spirit is a lifestyle of taking ownership and using the gift of holy spirit. And elevating spiritual knowledge above natural knowledge.

Romans 8:4–8:

That the righteousness of the law might be fulfilled in us, who walk not after the flesh,[29] but after the Spirit.[30]

---

29 Those living, assessing, and distinguishing issues by the five bodily senses only, or natural knowledge.

30 Those living, assessing, and distinguishing issues by the revealed Word of God, thereby elevating spiritual knowledge above natural knowledge.

For they that are after the flesh do mind the things of the flesh; but they that are after the Spirit the things of the Spirit.

For to be carnally minded *is* death; but to be spiritually minded *is* life and peace.

Because the carnal mind *is* enmity against God: for it is not subject to the law of God [God's Word], neither indeed can be. So then they that are in the flesh cannot please God.

We don't want to walk by the flesh or our five senses and obey men. We want to walk by the spirit and obey God.

Romans 8:13–15:

For if ye live after the flesh, ye shall die: but if ye through the Spirit do mortify the deeds of the body, ye shall live.

For as many as are led by the Spirit of God, they are the sons of God.

For ye have not received the spirit of bondage again to fear; but ye have received the Spirit of adoption [sonship by God], whereby we cry, Abba, Father.

The evil spirit of bondage noted in this section is not from the true God but comes from Satan. This spirit of bondage specializes in binding and tethering God's people to an earthly identity, the opposite of a heavenly identity in Christ. Binding a child of God to an earthly identity negates the impact of the work of Christ. The truth of being seated at God's right hand with Christ in heaven and having eternal life is brushed aside for an earthly identity.

Careers, hobbies, relationships, family background, social standing, and education are all part of life. There is nothing wrong with them in and of themselves. They all have the potential to enrich our lives.

However, it is when the child of God *identifies* with any of these uniquely and exclusively above who they are in Christ that they become *earthly bound.*

Our identity (who we really are) is what influences and directs our purpose and meaning for living. When something other than Christ becomes our source of identity, circumstances, and choices, good or bad, begin to define who we are rather than obstacles to be overcome and successes to be enjoyed. Someone's identity can be evidenced in what they say, do, and decide. To identify with the flesh produces fear because the flesh has an end in death, but the holy spirit is eternal. This fear binds the believer, so living and speaking for the true God grinds to a halt. Freedom in Christ and the glory that awaits the Christian believer at the return of Christ is replaced with unending captivity and oppression due to fear of death.

Hebrews 2:15:

And deliver them who through fear of death were all their lifetime subject to bondage.

Galatians 5:1:

Stand fast therefore in the liberty [freedom] wherewith Christ hath made us free, and be not entangled again with the yoke of bondage.

The word "bondage" in Romans 8:15, Hebrews 2:15, and Galatians 5:1 is derived from the Greek word *doulos*, meaning "a slave, one bound to serve," hence bondage and enslavement. Our desire according to our new nature is to walk in the freedom we have in Christ. Our heavenly identity in Christ is the key to unlocking this freedom.

More Than a Conqueror

Claiming our justification through the faith of Jesus Christ is our foundation upon which we are more than a conqueror over any fear because we refuse to leave ourselves open to all those judgments. We have only one judge and that is God. It is He who made us acceptable to Him (Ephesians 1:6).

Romans 8:30:

Moreover whom he did predestinate, them he also called: and whom he called, them he also justified [God's legal decision to justify man]: and whom he justified, them he also glorified [our being spiritually at one with God and future glory in Christ].

When we walk with that faith of Jesus Christ in our hearts, being justified, we look to the glory that is to be revealed at the return of Jesus Christ. This is what lives in our souls. As this truth does, the prison bars of fear vanish.

Romans 8:31–33:

What shall we then say to these things? If God *be* for us, who *can be* against us?

He that spared not his own Son, but delivered him up for us all, how shall he not with him also freely give us all things?

Who shall lay anything to the charge of God's elect? *It is* God that justifieth.

Absolutely! If God has already justified us through the faith of Jesus Christ, then it's finished. We are complete in Christ. There is no more judgment! There is no more criticism. And we don't give in to the carnal

Christian, the world, or even our own selves because God has justified us through the faith of Jesus Christ.

Romans 8:34:

Who *is* he that condemneth? *It is* [31] Christ that died, yea rather, that is risen again, who is even at the right hand of God, who also maketh intercession for us.

If Christ died, rose, and intercedes with his position and life-giving authority at God's right hand for us, will he condemn us? The answer is clearly no.

If we ever might think that anyone has the right to condemn us before God, we must think again. Paul is making the point clearly that no one, not even Jesus Christ, is going to condemn us after he redeemed us. So, does anyone have the right to condemn us? NO! Absolutely not!

Jesus Christ's position at the right hand of God is above all the earthly bondage. He is our present representation of the authority and heavenly dignity we were given by God. As stated in Ephesians 1:19 and 20: *And what is the exceeding greatness of his power toward us who believe, according to the working of his mighty power. Which he wrought in Christ, when he raised him from the dead, and set* him *at his own right hand in the heavenly places.* This is our identity in Christ and all he accomplished.

Seated in heaven as the head of the Body, Christ anchors that position for us. And the life of God flows through him to the Body. He also intercedes with his position, not in active participation in the daily affairs of the church, but in representing the authority of God to give the life of God to others. This life and authority of God is held by Christ

---

31 It is good to note that The King James version often italicizes words added by the translators for clarity to aid the reader. However, these words may not have corresponding words in the source texts from where they were translated.

in heaven and extended to cover us who are *spiritually* seated with him while still *physically* on earth. We are his ambassadors with the authority to share the life of God through Christ to all the world until his return.

What about circumstantial obstacles? Are we going to allow the challenges and circumstances we face to define our lives? Are we going to punish ourselves by accepting these obstacles as some sort of "payment" for what we may have done or not done in our lives? NO! A THOUSAND TIMES, NO!

Romans 8:35–37:

> Who shall separate us from the love of Christ? *shall* tribulation, or distress, or persecution, or famine, or nakedness, or peril, or sword?
>
> As it is written, For thy sake we are killed all the day long; we are accounted as sheep for the slaughter.
>
> Nay, in all these things we are more than conquerors through him that loved us.

Sons of God deserve the dignity of being more than conquerors, not the shame of victimization. The idea represented in the phrase that we are "killed all the day long" is equivalent to the victim mentality so prevalent today. It is nothing new. Those who mentally set their feet in the concrete of the faith of Jesus Christ realize that they are justified by God and are less likely to fall into the victim trap. Anyone can be a victim of circumstances but to perpetually identify oneself as a victim produces an untenable situation for the Christian because this identity negates the truth that Christ was raised from the dead. Death, as the ultimate circumstance, was conquered at the resurrection.

Our God-given justification is part of the foundation upon which the more-than-a-conqueror mindset is built. When that foundation erodes, we see believers lose that mindset and fall prey to victimization.

No one disputes that life has challenges. But how we face them, with or without Christ, determines the outcome.

The close of the eighth chapter of Romans contrasts a victimization mindset with a more-than-a-conqueror mindset. The victim loses the boldness in Christ Jesus and the courage to live for God. This happens when the foundation of justification through the faith of Jesus Christ has been eroded, and a person seeks justification from some source other than God through Christ. Victimization is characterized by obeying men rather than God when men contradict God. Romans is the foundational discourse for this Age of Grace. And like two bookends, obedience to the household of faith is found in the first and last chapters of this book. How tremendous is this truth!

Obedience to the Household of Faith Bookends Romans

Romans 16:25–26:

Now to him that is of power to stablish you according to my gospel, and the preaching of Jesus Christ, according to the revelation of the mystery, which was kept secret since the world began,

But now is made manifest, and by the scriptures of the prophets, according to the commandment of the everlasting God, made known to all nations for the obedience [*hupakoē*-noun form of verb *hupakouō*] of faith [the household of faith].

Obedience to the household of faith should be spread to all the nations. Obedience to the household of faith is first seen in Romans 1:5 and then again here in Romans 16:26. This concept bookends the doctrinal foundation of the Age of Grace—Romans. Obedience to the household of faith is about obeying God rather than men and accepting only God's judgment because we have been justified through the faith of

Jesus Christ. With such truth living in our hearts, we can say goodbye to being victims and embrace a more-than-a-conqueror mindset. We are bold. We speak forth the Word, and we live for God regardless of any judgment that comes. Our identity is in Christ, not in anyone or anything of the earth.

From a practical perspective, the early followers of Christ were living truths later recorded in Romans by the Apostle Paul. For example, Romans 1:5 and 16:26 both note obedience regarding the faith. In both these verses, the word "obedience" is an action noun that embodies its heritage as a verb. The word "faith" is receiving the action of this obedience. In other words, what were they to obey? They were to obey the faith.

This practice of obeying the faith was very much a part of the early church, though it had not yet been written. By the time Romans was written around 58 A.D., obedience to the household of faith was already part of the early believers' lifestyle. The believers were practicing this obedience based on what the first apostles taught. This is even before the term "Christians" came into use (Acts 11:26). Concepts often develop along these lines. Actions are identified with words and then develop into concepts later.

The Early Christians and the Household of Faith

Acts 6:7:

And the word of God increased; and the number of the disciples multiplied in Jerusalem greatly; and a great company of the priests [Judeans] were obedient [*hupakouō*] to the faith.

Acts 6 identifies the first reference to "the faith" or the household of faith because all the believers, as a family, were obeying the same thing.

In context, we see significant points to help us understand what the early church understood and how they functioned.

The word "obedient" is the Greek word *hupakouō*. As we have seen, it is a verb form of the noun *hupakoē*. The verb *hupakouō* means to hear, but it also carries a sense of stillness or attention with the expectation that one answers. The words "multiplied [*plēthunō*] . . . greatly" indicate the interest generated in Christ and his accomplished work. Many became adherents. The word "increased" is the Greek word *auxanō*. This Greek word is used of plant growth, as well as natural and spiritual human development that reflects an unforced organic growth from within. When used of human spiritual growth, it is a result of walking well-pleasing to God and ". . . being fruitful in every good work, and increasing [*auxanō*] in the knowledge of God." (Colossians 1:10)

What is so interesting about the words "increased," "multiplied," and "obedience" in Acts 6:7 is that they all are translations of Greek verbs, therefore describing the actions of the early Christians. The Greek grammatical construction of these words describes continual action in the past. All three of these continual actions are linked. The growth of the Word in believers' lives, the multiplying of disciples, and the obedience to the faith are all tied together. These three early Christian actions are interdependently bound and exemplary of true Christian action.

To further draw our attention to this verse, Acts 6:7 is a figure of speech called *symperasma*, a concluding summary. This verse concludes and summarizes accounts of the early Christians up to this point in the written record of the Book of Acts. This is quite revealing because these accounts chronicle practical truths regarding obedience to the household of faith. We can see truths the early Christians lived that characterize obedience to the household faith. Like taking ownership and using the gift of holy spirit to help others. And elevating spiritual knowledge above natural knowledge. In Chapter 3, Peter and John went to the temple and ministered healing to a man who was lame from his mother's womb.

Healing of the Man at the Temple Gate

Acts 3:4–7:

And Peter, fastening his eyes upon him with John, said, Look on us.

And he gave heed unto them, expecting to receive something of them.

Then Peter said, Silver and gold have I none; but such as I have give I thee: In the name of Jesus Christ of Nazareth rise up and walk.

And he [Peter] took him by the right hand, and lifted *him* up: and immediately his feet and ankle bones received strength.

This record highlights the lifestyle of walking by the spirit functioning in the early church. Peter and John took ownership of the gift and elevated the spiritual knowledge from God above the natural knowledge in the situation. They were fully persuaded and expected that this man could be healed in the name of Jesus Christ even though he was lame from his mother's womb. This is another example of obeying God as He worked in them to produce healing.

This situation with the man at the Temple gate got the attention of the religious people. When the apostles were challenged about their authority and the nature of this healing, they spoke boldly. That's part of being obedient to the faith—because they stood on the faith of Jesus Christ that had justified them.

Acts 4:10–13:

Be it known unto you all, and to all the people of Israel, that by the name of Jesus Christ of Nazareth, whom ye crucified, whom God raised from the dead, *even* by him doth this man stand here before you whole.

This is the stone which was set at nought of you builders, which is become the head of the corner.

Neither is there salvation in any other: for there is none other name under heaven given among men, whereby we must be saved.

Now when they saw the boldness of Peter and John, and perceived that they were unlearned and ignorant men, they marveled; and they took knowledge of them, that they had been with Jesus.

Peter and John were not afraid to speak for God. The religious leaders were trying to stop them from living for the true God and from speaking His Word. They were trying to bring them into bondage, but the apostles did not succumb. They had a more-than-a-conqueror mindset.

Acts 4:19–20:

But Peter and John answered and said unto them, Whether it be right in the sight of God to hearken unto you more than unto God, judge ye.

For we cannot but speak the things which we have seen and heard.

The conviction of truth was a fire burning within them like Jeremiah the prophet wrote, ". . . But his word was in mine heart as a burning fire shut up in my bones, and I was weary with forbearing, and I could not stay." (Jeremiah 20:9) Jeremiah couldn't hold back from speaking the Word, because it was a living fire ablaze within him.

Acts 4:21–24:

So when they had further threatened them, they let them go, finding nothing how they might punish them, because of the people [public opinion can be a powerful tool]: for all *men* glorified God for that which was done.

For the man was above forty years old, on whom this miracle of healing was shewed.

And being let go, they went to their own company, and reported all that the chief priests and elders had said unto them.

And when they heard that, they lifted up their voice to God with one accord, and said . . .

They lifted their voice with one accord in prayer. "One accord" is that Greek word *homothumadon*, which means they exhibited one *passion* to move with God. They were unified, and their prayer evidenced their willingness to get God involved. Involving God is a great lesson of truth in times of need (Hebrews 4:16).

Acts 4:29:

And now, Lord, behold their threatenings: and grant unto thy servants, that with all boldness they may speak thy word.

Threats of punishment come from those who lord over God's people. These threats can be intimidating. They can mentally incarcerate people and make them afraid to live for the true God or speak for Him. Such control via intimidation can stop believers from walking out on the Word and from walking by the spirit. It is bondage. But the apostles would have none of this.

Acts 4:30–31:

By stretching forth thine hand to heal; and that signs and wonders may be done by the name of thy holy child Jesus.

And when they had prayed, the place was shaken where they were assembled together; and they were all filled with the Holy Ghost, and they spake the word of God with boldness.

Following this prayer, they spoke boldly. Speaking boldly on behalf of Christ in the face of condemnation and judgment of others is a characteristic of God's love in us in its most mature expression. This truth was later recorded by the Apostle John.

I John 4:17–18:

Herein is our love made perfect, that we may have boldness in the day of judgment [man's day]: because as he is, so are we in this world.[32]

There is no fear in love; but perfect love casteth out fear: because fear hath torment. He that feareth is not made perfect in love.

---

32 Some read this verse and think it is speaking about having boldness in some future time of judgment. This is not a precise understanding. This day of judgment is equivalent to I Corinthians 4:3, "man's judgment [day]," in which man does the judging today. The same applies in I John 4:17 because the Greek verbs "made perfect . . . are," referring to the believers, take place in this world and are present tense or have their impact in the present, not the future. For verb forms, see endnote for Barbara Friberg, Timothy Friberg, *Analytical Greek New Testament*, p. 728.

The fallout from healing the man at the Temple gate continued to upset the religious leaders. Yet the apostles did not hesitate to preach and teach in the name of Jesus Christ.

Acts 5:28–32:

Saying, Did not we straitly command you that ye should not teach in this name? and, behold, ye have filled Jerusalem with your doctrine, and intend to bring this man's blood upon us.

Then Peter and the *other* apostles answered and said, We ought to obey God rather than men.

The God of our fathers raised up Jesus, whom ye slew and hanged on a tree.

Him hath God exalted with his right hand *to be* a Prince and a Saviour, for to give repentance to Israel, and forgiveness of sins.

And we are his witnesses of these things; and so is also the Holy Ghost,[33] whom God hath given to them that obey him.

The apostles boldly responded with this tremendous comeback: "We ought to obey God rather than men." This is the challenge set before us all when it comes to obedience to the faith.

Natural man will never acknowledge the accomplished work of the Son of God. He who offered his sinless life for the whole world and paved the way for eternal life. Natural men often condemn and judge such obedience to God because they do not understand it.

---

33 The "Holy Ghost" here refers to the gift of holy spirit, which all Christians have, yet not all take it as their own and use it. When the gift is personally used, it produces evidence to others of the power given through Christ and is the witness, like is seen here with the healing of the lame man in Acts 3. This is what stirred the opposition.

Family First, Function Second

Obedience to God rather than men is the very core of obedience to the household of faith. By standing on our justification through the faith of Jesus Christ, we can speak the gospel of his salvation boldly. With this also comes the ability to handle growth and change within the Christian ministry, because we navigate with mutual respect in the household.

In the previous chapter, for example, we learned how the first-century believers handled the business of caring for physical needs and still maintained teaching the Word. In Acts 6:2–6, there were specific people who stood out for their service in the household of faith. Obedience to the faith is the environment that allows strengths and functions of service to emerge.

We are not intimidated by each other or in competition with each other. Why? Because we each have the same measure of faith, which is the faith of Jesus Christ (Romans 12:3). We want each believer to function spiritually.

The household faith is so important because it captures the spiritual equality each family member has in God's sight due to the measure of faith. The faith of Christ is where we find equality in God's family. No one receives more, no one receives less. Genuine respect is built one for another. Obedience to the household faith is when believers hearken and submit to God's design and treat one another accordingly. This is obeying God rather than men.

In the Body of Christ is where we find equality in *importance*, but not in *function* (Romans 12:4). This is the best spiritual atmosphere for growth and for moving the Word from generation to generation. Family first, function second. In this environment, young people grow and develop their strengths according to the Word. There is no need to squelch younger believers and leaders. We want to guide, encourage, and support them.

Obedience to the household of faith is also about winning in the spiritual competition. We fight for our brothers and sisters and not against them. Obedience to the faith removes us from a self-centered life to a Christ-centered life. Obedience to the faith starts with us individually, but it is not just about us.

Galatians 6:10:

As we have therefore opportunity, let us do good unto all *men,* especially unto them who are of the household of [the] faith.

We are to be good to all people with special awareness and care for the brethren of the household of faith. God put us into a household so we can help each other grow in Christ. Everybody deserves that because everybody has a treasure in an earthen vessel that the excellency of the power may be of God and not of us (II Corinthians 4:7). We desire each member of the family to rise to their potential in Christ.

Colossians 1:27–29:

To whom God would make known what is the riches of the glory of this mystery among the Gentiles; which is Christ in you, the hope of glory:

Whom we preach [to bring home to anyone], warning every man, and teaching every man in all wisdom; that we may present every man perfect [mature, in ESV] in Christ Jesus:

Whereunto I also labour, striving according to his working, which worketh in me mightily.

"Every man" means everyone. No one gets missed! We labor toward such an environment where everyone can grow in Christ (Ephesians

4:16). We want to see people mature and stand in Christ, and it starts with that foundation of obedience to the household of faith. Family first, function second.

Made Known to All Nations

As mentioned, Romans is the foundational treatise for the Age of Grace. And it is bookended in the first and last chapters by obedience to the household of faith. Romans declares that obedience to the household of faith should be spread to all the nations. Obedience to the household of faith is about obeying God rather than men and accepting only God's judgment. We are bold, we speak forth the Word, and we live for God, regardless of any judgment from carnal Christians or man's judgment or even ourselves.

In Ephesus, the Apostle Paul taught the revelation of the mystery of the Body of Christ. The foundation of this was obedience to the household of faith. The gospel spread throughout the entire area of Asia Minor to such an extent that God declared, *So mightily grew the word of God and prevailed* (Acts 19:20). What a testimony!

Yet by the end of Paul's life, as recorded in II Timothy, all Asia Minor had turned away from him, meaning the truths he taught. This loss to Christianity cannot be overstated. Soon after, sects and splinter groups developed and changed the true doctrine of the household of faith and the Body of Christ as originally taught. Instead:

- Justification through works of men, not grace, replaced the faith of Jesus Christ.
- Future judgment replaced the truth of the glorious return of Christ.
- Fear and uncertainty replaced love and joy.

Such spiritual degradation became the norm, casting a dark shadow over the gospel. Such spiritual ruin is not acceptable in our day and time. We must stand up together to advance the truth of the gospel!

Philippians 1:27–28:

Only let your conversation [We are seated in heaven and therefore citizens of heaven; to be a free citizen and live as such] be as it becometh the gospel of Christ: that whether I come and see you, or else be absent, I may hear of your affairs, that ye stand fast [standing firm, in ESV] in one spirit, with one mind striving together for the faith [the household of faith] of the gospel;

And in nothing terrified by your adversaries: which is to them an evident token [a pointing out with the finger, an indicating] of perdition, but to you of salvation, and that of God.

Every time we stand firmly obedient and strive together for the household of faith, we are obeying God rather than men. Every time we accept God's justification through the faith of Jesus Christ, we are obeying God rather than men. Every time we speak boldly for God and walk by the spirit, we are obeying God rather than men. Such unified spiritual declarations emphasize the adversary's destruction and our salvation.

Obedience to the household of faith is characterized by obeying God rather than men. It is about walking by the spirit and not by the flesh or falling prey to the judgments of men that overrule God. Obedience to the household of faith conveys a "respect came upon every soul" attitude. Knowing we all have the "Christ in you" treasure in earthen vessels promotes an environment where spiritual strengths and functions can flourish.

May God in His infinite grace and mercy preserve and prosper this understanding among His people through our Lord Jesus Christ.

CONCLUSION

In this book, we found insight into the ongoing spiritual fight, the struggle that rages between truth and its antagonists. Whenever and wherever Christian believers find themselves faced with false accusations, threats, and intimidation, these truths will help them navigate a way out. This book is a clear road map of how to move ahead with grace and keep the faith when leaders we look to fail by compromising on their spiritual calling and pursue a worldly application of Christianity. Leaders fail when they resist God and turn to practices that glorify men. This biblically immoral decision is what produces the Christian leadership dilemma.

Whether you are realizing you have been on a personal detour from the things of God or just starting out in the Christian experience, the grace of God in Christ Jesus is the fertile soil in which the understanding of the household of faith and functioning in love can flourish. A central theme is the idea of providing answers when accusations are directed toward anyone endeavoring to speak truth to a resistant authority or power.

Respect and dignity are the cornerstones of any biblical relationship. In biblical relationships, someone winning does not mean someone else must lose. True relationships are about "win-win" situations. We want to build up each other, not tear each other down to elevate ourselves. The basis of this approach is respect for God and what He wrought in Christ in us.

Obedience to the household of faith is the lamp that every Christian believer can use to navigate their journey in life. Within this journey is the concept of *homothumadon*—the like-minded passion available to follow any movement of God in any day and time.

For this to be realized, it is vital to the life of a Christian community to have quality leaders who work together with God and His people. Leaders of character that navigate themselves according to what God says as opposed to what men say. God expects His people to work in unity with Him and not stray into their own pursuits or worldly ethics that are often outside of His purposes, guidance, and inspiration.

God knows how to work with each of us and not overstep His boundaries. He does not control us or force our decisions. He may, in His wisdom, lay out our options. The job of a godly leader is to treat people with similar respect and allow them the same freedom to choose.

Summary

Jesus Christ, the Apostle Paul, and the Apostle Peter all denounced the practice of lording over God's people, otherwise known as "top-down leadership." Top-down leadership occurs when people impose their will upon others from a position of leverage for personal gain. Often this is done through the narrow lens of egocentricity. This behavior oversteps a leader's God-given role, which should be Christ-centered.

Sometimes Christian leaders cross the line and infringe on the free will of others. We are all fallible and may not always put forth our best efforts. However, this must not become habitual. If left unchecked, this overstep generates the temptation to lord over God's people. In contrast, Christian leaders should be servants, helpers of others' joy, and willing examples of teaching and guiding others.

How do we deal with disagreement and conflict among Christian believers? How do we proceed when there appears to be an impasse? Do we argue about who is right? Do we delve into "Whose side are you on?" Certainly, it is acceptable to have opinions on certain topics, but not about what God declares is right or wrong. Morality and preference should never be misconstrued as one and the same. What God declares is right or wrong is truth. When we stand with God on His Word, everything else tends to sort itself out.

"Who is right?" or "Who do you stand with?" leads us to focus on people and can fuel division. The correct response is "God and His Word are right" and "I stand with God and what He says is right." Any impasse becomes less difficult to traverse when the light of the Word is introduced into the situation.

In considering the Greek word *homothumadon*, we identified a unique characteristic among the first-century Christians that can help us as we move forward. We saw the meaning of this word is to have "one accord" or "one mind, unanimously." Rarely do we see such agreements among men because men do not start with God's heart and wisdom. Reaching this one mind is not done by five-senses agreements of men, but rather is purposed in God, aided, and guided by Him. As believers, our success in reaching one accord is measured by our willingness to get God involved. It can only be accomplished with God.

A movement of God is evident in each of the seven positive occurrences of this word in the Book of Acts and results in unity of purpose and action from believers. These movements set the practical foundation for the church and, in some cases, showed their response to conflict. The leaders played a key role. It was with their energy of conviction that each leader recognized God at work. Then leaders inspired and guided followers as a team. Each member of the team added their own personal energy of conviction, enthusiasm, and commitment to what God was moving.

The Christian ministry, simply stated, involves any service and labor performed on behalf of Christ and that lines up with God's Word. How do we keep the Word first in our service? It is by being obedient to the household faith. Obedience begins with maintaining that genuine respect in Christ for others in God's family, including respect for ourselves. Our identity in Christ should be treasured in each of us. As we each individually recognize these truths and embrace them as God's Word, we can then help others.

Obedience to the household of faith centers on obeying God rather than men. The underpinnings of obeying God are to submit to His accomplished work in Christ for us and in us. This unmerited divine favor is grace. It involves accepting, as our own, the work of another, namely Jesus Christ. This is our identity in Christ.

In contrast, obeying men is to submit to the judgment, identity, and work and will of men when grace in Christ is offered. Grace is what guides believers to identify with Christ as sons of God, eternal and seated in heaven. Works of men herd people like cattle and intimidate them in the opposite direction to identify with the efforts of men, earthly bound and temporal. Understanding grace requires humility to God and His revealed Word. It glorifies Him.

Every time we stand firmly obedient and strive together for the household of faith, we are obeying God rather than men. Every time we accept only the justification that comes from God through the faith of Jesus Christ, we are obeying God rather than men. Every time we speak for God boldly and walk by the spirit, we are obeying God rather than men. Such unified spiritual claims point out the adversary's *destruction* and our *salvation*.

Final Thoughts

In the beginning of the Christian church, followers met with little resistance. The fledgling church enjoyed a brief time before Satan, the supposed god of this world, or age, marshaled opposition through indignant religious leaders. These worldly men, cloaked in religious garb, were agents of evil setting the stage for the spiritual drama still playing today: obeying men rather than obeying God, the Christian leadership dilemma. Obedience to the household of faith carries an attitude of "respect . . . upon every soul," that recognizes the treasure in earthen vessels of "Christ in you." This attitude stands in direct opposition to the commandments of men.

At the end of the Apostle Paul's life, he wrote these words in II Timothy 4:7: "I have fought a good fight, I have finished my course, I have kept the faith." To keep the faith is to obey the faith. Paul kept the faith of Jesus Christ individually and promoted the household of faith collectively among God's people, the family of God. Paul understood that obedience to the household of faith is the practical foundation upon which the Body of Christ truly functions, preserving the integrity of truth and freedom in the Christian ministry. Obedience to the faith begins with mutual respect based on the accomplished work of Christ. It is his work that allows us to move ahead with grace and keep the faith even in the wake of our own moral failures or those of others.

When grace is not involved, actions that appear dutiful can simply become the works of men. Why? Because the actions are not resting upon the only foundation worth building on, the Lord Jesus Christ.

The key is keeping the right heart or attitude; otherwise, we become self-absorbed, and God and His Word are not involved.

When we are selfless, or Christ-centered, our thankful and cheerful hearts are in our giving. There is profit, and godly service results. This is good fruit. When we are self-absorbed and self-serving, service becomes obligatory and religious. Comparison and accusations result. This is bad fruit.

The following section has already been handled in this book. But the lessons here are so simple, profound, and far-reaching, that I thought it was worth repeating.

Luke 10:38–42:

Now it came to pass, as they went, that he entered into a certain village: and a certain woman named Martha received him into her house.

And she had a sister called Mary, which also sat at Jesus' feet, and heard his word.

But Martha was cumbered about much serving, and came to him, and said, Lord, dost thou not care that my sister hath left me to serve alone? bid her therefore that she help me.

And Jesus answered and said unto her, Martha, Martha, thou art careful and troubled about many things:

But one thing is needful: and Mary hath chosen that good part, which shall not be taken away from her.

Luke is the only gospel account that records this event, making it uniquely significant. Martha was cumbered or distracted and accused Jesus of not caring. She then accused Mary of being unwilling to help. Once Martha was done accusing, she began to direct the lives of others, like commanding Jesus to direct Mary to support her.

For the unsaved, making Jesus Lord is how someone becomes born-again and receives eternal life. For the saved, making Jesus Christ Lord is to engage in a life of service. What we must guard against is self-absorbed service which, though appearing pious, promotes the work but loses the heart of service, just like Martha.

Martha had forgotten the Word of the Lord that Jesus was delivering even though he was in the flesh in her own home delivering it. Sometimes the answers we need are right in front of us, but we are too distracted with our own pursuits that we miss them. Jesus Christ lovingly addressed Martha's anxiety and redirected her: "But one thing is needful: and Mary hath chosen that good part." Mary chose correctly. There are many things in life to distract us, but Mary chose the Word of the Lord embodied in Jesus Christ.

Are you "careful and troubled about many things"? The answer you are seeking is simple—choose the "one thing [that] is needful . . . that good part," which is Jesus Christ.

This section illustrates the central issue in our discussion, Jesus Christ as declared in the Word of God. God is the *why* of life. He provides meaning and purpose for our lives. Jesus Christ is the *how* of life. He is the vital connection and access that explains how to practically live the life God wants for you. We have a choice upon what foundation we will build our lives—the world's way or God's way.

I Corinthians 3:10-11:

According to the grace of God which is given unto me, as a wise masterbuilder, I have laid the foundation, and another buildeth thereon. But let every man take heed how he buildeth thereupon.

For other foundation can no man lay than that is laid, which is Jesus Christ.

We are not victims—we choose how to live our lives. We are not to be sheep led to the slaughter, but we are more than conquerors through Him that loved us (Romans 8:36–37).

Let us each choose "that good part" as we sojourn in this life and help as many others as we can along our journey. In so doing, we will contribute to the solution of the ages, which is God's answer for all questions of the heart, deliverance from all physical and mental ailments, and victory amid all challenges.

Only God provides the ultimate and conclusive resolution to man's struggle. Within the revelation of the church in the Age of Grace is the spiritual cohesion that can bind men's hearts together regardless of race, socioeconomic background, education, or citizenship.

God can guide us into this spiritual unity that is pure, incorruptible, and indeed transcends this brief life on earth. This is our desired destination, living in the truth regarding the grace of God embodied in the accomplished work of our risen and returning Lord and Savior, Jesus Christ.

Resolving the Christian leadership dilemma starts with each of us. When church leaders fail, let us not sit idle or retreat to a shell of anonymity and blend into worldly shadows. Let us shine as beacons in this life by moving ahead with God's grace and keeping the faith. And let us help as many others as we can do the same.

Matthew 5:14–16:

Ye are the light of the world. A city that is set on a hill cannot be hid.

Neither do men light a candle, and put it under a bushel, but on a candlestick; and it giveth light unto all that are in the house.

Let your light so shine before men, that they may see your good works, and glorify your Father which is in heaven.

May God in His infinite grace and mercy preserve and prosper this understanding of obedience to the household of faith and the interdependence we all share in the Body of Christ among His people.

ABOUT THE AUTHOR

F.D. Magnelli has been a minister for over three decades and has labored in local congregations as well as in corporate administration for Christian organizations and networks with Christian leaders domestically and abroad. He has developed and continues to teach biblical education courses live and online and travels nationally and internationally. He has baccalaureate degrees in political science and theology and a master's degree in education. F.D. resides in Melbourne, Florida.

ENDNOTES

Introduction

James Strong, *The Exhaustive Concordance of The Bible*, Macdonald
Publishing Company, Maclean, VA, 1890, p. 546.

George V. Wigram, Ralph D. Winter, *The Word Study Concordance*,
Tyndale House Publishers, Inc., Wheaton, IL, 1972, p. 74.

Joseph H. Thayer, *Thayer's Greek-English Lexicon of the New Testament*,
Hendrickson Publishers, Inc., Peabody, MA, 1996, p. 65.

Chapter 1

Ethelbert W. Bullinger, *A Critical Lexicon and Concordance to the
English and Greek New Testament*, Zondervan Publishing House,
Grand Rapids, MI, 1975, p. 317.

George V. Wigram, Ralph D. Winter, *The Word Study Concordance*,
Tyndale House Publishers, Inc., Wheaton, IL, 1972, p. 436.

Ethelbert W. Bullinger, *A Critical Lexicon and Concordance to the
English and Greek New Testament*, Zondervan Publishing House,
Grand Rapids, MI, 1975, p. 468.

Ibid., p. 69.

George Ricker Berry, *The Interlinear Literal Translation of the Greek New Testament,* Zondervan Publishing House, Grand Rapids, MI, 1979, p. 470.

A.T. Robertson, *A Grammar of the Greek New Testament in the Light of Historical Research,* Broadman Press, Nashville, TN, 1934, p. 895.

Thomas Jefferson Memorial Inscriptions Rotunda, excerpted from a letter from Thomas Jefferson to Dr. Benjamin Rush, 23 September 1800. Retrieved November 28, 2019, from https://www.nps.gov/thje/learn/photosmultimedia/quotations.htm.

The Comparative Study Bible, The Zondervan Corporation, Grand Rapids, MI, 1984, p. 2,866.

Ethelbert W. Bullinger, *A Critical Lexicon and Concordance to the English and Greek New Testament,* Zondervan Publishing House, Grand Rapids, MI, 1975, p. 989.

Ibid., p. 371.

James MacGregor Burns, *Leadership,* Harper & Rowe, Publishers, Inc., New York, NY, 1978, p. 4.

David Alan Black, *It's Still Greek to Me: An Easy-to-Understand Guide to Intermediate Greek,* Baker Books, Grand Rapids, MI, 1998, p. 84.

Joseph H. Thayer, *Thayer's Greek-English Lexicon of the New Testament,* Hendrickson Publishers, Inc., Peabody, MA, 1996, p. 332.

Ethelbert W. Bullinger, *A Critical Lexicon and Concordance to the English and Greek New Testament,* Zondervan Publishing House, Grand Rapids, MI, 1975, p. 252.

J.D. Douglas, F.F. Bruce, J.I. Packer, N. Hillyer, D. Guthrie, A.R. Millard, D.J. Wiseman, *New Bible Dictionary, Second Edition,* InterVarsity Press, Leicester, England, Tyndale House Publishers, Inc., Wheaton, IL, 1982, p. 690.

Ethelbert W. Bullinger, *A Critical Lexicon and Concordance to the English and Greek New Testament,* Zondervan Publishing House, Grand Rapids, MI, 1975, p. 280.

Ibid., pp. 471, 624.

George Ricker Berry, *The Interlinear Literal Translation of the Greek New Testament*, Zondervan Publishing House, Grand Rapids, MI, 1979, p. 428.

H.C. Andersen (1837). *The Emperor's New Clothes.* Retrieved November 30, 2019, http://andersen.sdu.dk/vaerk/hersholt/TheEmperorsNewClothes_e.html.

Chapter 2

The Comparative Study Bible, The Zondervan Corporation, Grand Rapids, MI, 1984, p. 2,971.

Joseph H. Thayer, *Thayer's Greek-English Lexicon of the New Testament*, Hendrickson Publishers, Inc., Peabody, MA, 1996, p. 56.

The Comparative Study Bible, The Zondervan Corporation, Grand Rapids, MI, 1984, p. 2,973.

Ethelbert W. Bullinger, *Figures of Speech Used in the Bible*, Baker Book House, Grand Rapids, MI, 1968, p. 307.

J.D. Douglas, F.F. Bruce, J.I. Packer, N. Hillyer, D. Guthrie, A.R. Millard, D.J. Wiseman, *New Bible Dictionary*, Second Edition, InterVarsity Press, Leicester, England, Tyndale House Publishers, Inc., Wheaton, IL, 1982, p. 210.

Harold K. Moulton, *The Analytical Greek Lexicon Revised*, Zondervan Publishing House, Grand Rapids, MI, 1978, p. 265.

Joseph H. Thayer, *Thayer's Greek-English Lexicon of the New Testament*, Hendrickson Publishers, Inc., Peabody, MA, 1996, p. 41.

Ethelbert W. Bullinger, *A Critical Lexicon and Concordance to the English and Greek New Testament*, Zondervan Publishing House, Grand Rapids, MI, 1975, p. 821.

Joseph H. Thayer, *Thayer's Greek-English Lexicon of the New Testament*, Hendrickson Publishers, Inc., Peabody, MA, 1996, p. 615.

Ethelbert W. Bullinger, *A Critical Lexicon and Concordance to the English and Greek New Testament*, Zondervan Publishing House, Grand Rapids, MI, 1975, p. 54.

Ibid., p. 584.

W.J. Conybeare, J.S. Howson, *The Life and Epistles of St. Paul*, Wm. B. Eerdmans Publishing Company, Grand Rapids, MI, 1949, p. 833.

George V. Wigram, Ralph D. Winter, *The Word Study Concordance*, Tyndale House Publishers, Inc., Wheaton, IL, 1972, p. 415.

Ethelbert W. Bullinger, *A Critical Lexicon and Concordance to the English and Greek New Testament*, Zondervan Publishing House, Grand Rapids, MI, 1975, p. 580.

Chapter 3

Ethelbert W. Bullinger, *A Critical Lexicon and Concordance to the English and Greek New Testament*, Zondervan Publishing House, Grand Rapids, MI, 1975, p. 24.

Retrieved May, 13, 2020 from https://www.biblestudytools.com/lexicons/greek/nas/ homothumadon.html.

George V. Wigram, Ralph D. Winter, *The Word Study Concordance*, Tyndale House Publishers, Inc., Wheaton, IL, 1972, pp. 530–531.

James Strong, *The Exhaustive Concordance of The Bible*, Macdonald Publishing Company, Maclean, VA, 1890, p. 52.

Ibid., p. 37.

Ethelbert W. Bullinger, *A Critical Lexicon and Concordance to the English and Greek New Testament*, Zondervan Publishing House, Grand Rapids, MI, 1975, p. 905.

James Strong, *The Exhaustive Concordance of The Bible*, Macdonald Publishing Company, Maclean, VA, 1890, p. 115.

Joseph H. Thayer, *Thayer's Greek-English Lexicon of the New Testament*, Hendrickson Publishers, Inc., Peabody, MA, 1996, p. 571.

Ethelbert W. Bullinger, *A Critical Lexicon and Concordance to the English and Greek New Testament*, Zondervan Publishing House, Grand Rapids, MI, 1975, p. 902.

Gerhard Kittel. *Theological Dictionary of the New Testament*, Wm. B. Eerdmans Publishing Company, Grand Rapids, MI, 1964, vol. 1, pp. 689–716.

W.E. Vine, Merrill F. Unger, William White, Jr., *Vine's Complete Expository Dictionary of Old and New Testament Words*, Thomas Nelson, Inc., Publishers, Nashville, TN, 1985, p. 249.

Finis Jennings Dake, *Dake's Annotated Reference Bible*, Dake Publishing, Inc., Lawrenceville, GA, 1999, p. 471.

Ibid., p. 292.

Joseph H. Thayer, *Thayer's Greek-English Lexicon of the New Testament*, Hendrickson Publishers, Inc., Peabody, MA, 1996, p. 370.

W.E. Vine, Merrill F. Unger, William White, Jr., *Vine's Complete Expository Dictionary of Old and New Testament Words*, Thomas Nelson, Inc., Publishers, Nashville, TN, 1985, p. 511.

Gerhard Kittel, *Theological Dictionary of the New Testament*, Wm. B. Eerdmans Publishing Company, Grand Rapids, MI., 1967, vol. 4, p. 5.

Ethelbert W. Bullinger, *A Critical Lexicon and Concordance to the English and Greek New Testament*, Zondervan Publishing House, Grand Rapids, MI, 1975, pp. 316–317.

Gerhard Kittel, *Theological Dictionary of the New Testament*, Wm. B. Eerdmans Publishing Company, Grand Rapids, MI, 1964, vol. 6, p. 724.

Weymouth Bible; English Standard Version of the Bible.

Joseph H. Thayer, *Thayer's Greek-English Lexicon of the New Testament*, Hendrickson Publishers, Inc., Peabody, MA, 1996, p. 126.

Harold K. Moulton, *The Analytical Greek Lexicon Revised*, Zondervan Publishing House, Grand Rapids, MI, 1978, p. 278.

Ibid., p. 371.

Gerhard Kittel, *Theological Dictionary of the New Testament*, Wm. B. Eerdmans Publishing Company, Grand Rapids, MI, 1964, vol. 7, pp. 888–889.

Barbara Friberg, Timothy Friberg, *Analytical Greek New Testament*, Baker Book House, Grand Rapids, MI, 1981, p. 376.

George Ricker Berry, *The Interlinear Literal Translation of the Greek New Testament*, Zondervan Publishing House, Grand Rapids, MI, 1979, p. 322.

Ethelbert W. Bullinger, *A Critical Lexicon and Concordance to the English and Greek New Testament*, Zondervan Publishing House, Grand Rapids, MI, 1975, p. 172.

J.D. Douglas, F.F. Bruce, J.I. Packer, N. Hillyer, D. Guthrie, A.R. Millard, D.J. Wiseman, *New Bible Dictionary*, Second Edition, InterVarsity Press, Leicester, England, Tyndale House Publishers, Inc., Wheaton, IL, 1982, p. 374.

Barbara Friberg, Timothy Friberg, *Analytical Greek New Testament*, Baker Book House, Grand Rapids, MI, 1981, p. 377.

Ethelbert W. Bullinger, *A Critical Lexicon and Concordance to the English and Greek New Testament*, Zondervan Publishing House, Grand Rapids, MI, 1975, p. 847.

Ethelbert W. Bullinger, *Number in Scripture, Its Supernatural Design and Spiritual Significance*, Kregel Publications, Grand Rapids, MI, 1967, p. 167.

Ethelbert W. Bullinger, *A Critical Lexicon and Concordance to the English and Greek New Testament*, Zondervan Publishing House, Grand Rapids, MI, 1975, p. 574.

Ibid., p. 182.

Joseph H. Thayer, *Thayer's Greek-English Lexicon of the New Testament*, Hendrickson Publishers, Inc., Peabody, MA, 1996, p. 28.

W.E. Vine, Merrill F. Unger, William White, Jr., *Vine's Complete Expository Dictionary of Old and New Testament Words*, Thomas Nelson, Inc., Publishers, Nashville, TN, 1985, p. 371.

Joseph H. Thayer, *Thayer's Greek-English Lexicon of the New Testament*, Hendrickson Publishers, Inc., Peabody, MA, 1996, p. 469.

Chapter 4

Joseph H. Thayer, *Thayer's Greek-English Lexicon of the New Testament*, Hendrickson Publishers, Inc., Peabody, MA, 1996, p. 137–138.

Ethelbert W. Bullinger, *A Critical Lexicon and Concordance to the English and Greek New Testament*, Zondervan Publishing House, Grand Rapids, MI, 1975, p. 197.

Barbara Friberg, Timothy Friberg, *Analytical Greek New Testament*, Baker Book House, Grand Rapids, MI, 1981, p. 220.

Ethelbert W. Bullinger, *A Critical Lexicon and Concordance to the English and Greek New Testament*, Zondervan Publishing House, Grand Rapids, MI, 1975, p. 134.

Joseph H. Thayer, *Thayer's Greek-English Lexicon of the New Testament*, Hendrickson Publishers, Inc., Peabody, MA, 1996, p. 349.

Ethelbert W. Bullinger, *Figures of Speech Used in the Bible, Baker Book House*, Grand Rapids, MI, 1968, p. 630.

Alfred Edersheim, *The Temple: Its Ministry and Services*, Hendrickson Publishers, Inc., Peabody, MA, 1994, pp. 206–207.

Ethelbert W. Bullinger, *A Critical Lexicon and Concordance to the English and Greek New Testament*, Zondervan Publishing House, Grand Rapids, MI, 1975, p. 624.

Gerhard Kittel, *Theological Dictionary of the New Testament*, Wm. B. Eerdmans Publishing Company, Grand Rapids, MI, 1964, vol. 1, p. 456.

Joseph H. Thayer, *Thayer's Greek-English Lexicon of the New Testament*, Hendrickson Publishers, Inc., Peabody, MA, 1996, p. 336.

Ethelbert W. Bullinger, *A Critical Lexicon and Concordance to the English and Greek New Testament*, Zondervan Publishing House, Grand Rapids, MI, 1975, p. 580.

Ibid., p. 311.

Ethelbert W. Bullinger, *Figures of Speech Used in the Bible*, Grand Rapids, MI, 1968, p. 657.

Barbara Friberg, Timothy Friberg, *Analytical Greek New Testament*, Baker Book House, Grand Rapids, MI, 1981, p. 382.

George V. Wigram, Ralph D. Winter, *The Word Study Concordance*, Tyndale House Publishers, Inc., Wheaton, IL, 1972, p. 80.

George Ricker Berry, *The Interlinear Literal Translation of the Greek New Testament*, Zondervan Publishing House, Grand Rapids, MI, 1979, p. 580.

Adam Clarke Commentaries. Retrieved December 7, 2019 from https://www. studylight.org/commentaries/acc/acts-6.html.

Ethelbert W. Bullinger, *Figures of Speech Used in the Bible*, Baker Book House, Grand Rapids, MI, 1968, p. 468.

Joseph H. Thayer, *Thayer's Greek-English Lexicon of the New Testament*, Hendrickson Publishers, Inc., Peabody, MA, 1996, p. 656.

Ethelbert W. Bullinger, *A Critical Lexicon and Concordance to the English and Greek New Testament*, Zondervan Publishing House, Grand Rapids, MI, 1975, p. 159.

A.T. Robertson, *A Grammar of the Greek New Testament in the Light of Historical Research*, Broadman Press, Nashville, TN, 1934, p. 882.

David Alan Black, *It's Still Greek to Me: An Easy-To-Understand Guide to Intermediate Greek*, Baker Books, Grand Rapids, MI, 1998, p. 106.

Barbara Friberg, Timothy Friberg, *Analytical Greek New Testament*, Baker Book House, Grand Rapids, MI, 1981, p. 370.

Ethelbert W. Bullinger, *A Critical Lexicon and Concordance to the English and Greek New Testament*, Zondervan Publishing House, Grand Rapids, MI, 1975, pp. 900–901.

The Comparative Study Bible, The Zondervan Corporation, Grand Rapids, MI, 1984, p. 2,768.

George Ricker Berry, *The Interlinear Literal Translation of the Greek New Testament*, Zondervan Publishing House, Grand Rapids, MI, 1979, p. 493.

Barbara Friberg, Timothy Friberg, *Analytical Greek New Testament*, Baker Book House, Grand Rapids, MI, 1981, p. 579.

A.T. Robertson, *A Grammar of the Greek New Testament in the Light of Historical Research*, Broadman Press, Nashville, TN, 1934, p. 895.

George Ricker Berry, *The Interlinear Literal Translation of the Greek New Testament*, Zondervan Publishing House, Grand Rapids, MI, 1979, p. 509.

Francis Brown, *The Brown-Driver-Briggs Hebrew and English Lexicon*, Hendrickson Publishers, Inc., Peabody, MA, 1996, p. 1,005.

Ibid, p. 744.

Ibid, p. 701.

Ethelbert W. Bullinger, *A Critical Lexicon and Concordance to the English and Greek New Testament*, Zondervan Publishing House, Grand Rapids, MI, 1975, p. 308.

Ibid p. 270.

W.E. Vine, Merrill F. Unger, William White, Jr., *Vine's Complete Expository Dictionary of Old and New Testament Words*, Thomas Nelson, Inc., Publishers, Nashville, TN, 1985, p. 220.

David McCullough, *John Adams*, Simon & Schuster, New York, NY, 2001, p. 29.

James M. Freeman, *Manners and Customs of the Bible*, Logos International, Plainfield, NJ, 1972, p. 17–18.

Edmund Burke (in a letter addressed to Thomas Mercer). Retrieved May 15, 2020 from www.openculture.com/2016/03/edmund-burkeon-in-action.html. Edmund Burke, "Thoughts on the Cause of the Present Discontents," 82–83 (1770) in: Select Works of Edmund Burke, vol. 1, p. 146 (Liberty Funded. 1999).

W.E. Vine, Merrill F. Unger, William White, Jr., *Vine's Complete Expository Dictionary of Old and New Testament Words*, Thomas Nelson, Inc., Publishers, Nashville, TN, 1985, p. 377.

Joseph H. Thayer, *Thayer's Greek-English Lexicon of the New Testament*, Hendrickson Publishers, Inc., Peabody, MA, 1996, p. 320.

Ethelbert W. Bullinger, *A Critical Lexicon and Concordance to the English and Greek New Testament*, Zondervan Publishing House, Grand Rapids, MI, 1975, p. 218.

Ethelbert W. Bullinger, *Figures of Speech Used in the Bible*, Baker Book House, Grand Rapids, MI, 1968, p. 726.

Chapter 5

Ethelbert W. Bullinger, *A Critical Lexicon and Concordance to the English and Greek New Testament*, Zondervan Publishing House, Grand Rapids, MI, 1975, p. 541.

Joseph H. Thayer, *Thayer's Greek-English Lexicon of the New Testament*, Hendrickson Publishers, Inc., Peabody, MA, 1996, p. 370.

Gerhard Kittel, *Theological Dictionary of the New Testament*, Wm. B. Eerdmans Publishing Company, Grand Rapids, MI, 1967, vol. 4, p. 5.

James Strong, *The Exhaustive Concordance of The Bible*, Macdonald Publishing Company, Maclean, VA, 1890, p. 34.

Joseph H. Thayer, *Thayer's Greek-English Lexicon of the New Testament*, Hendrickson Publishers, Inc., Peabody, MA, 1996, p. 141.

George Ricker Berry, *The Interlinear Literal Translation of the Greek New Testament*, Zondervan Publishing House, Grand Rapids, MI, 1979, p. 509.

James Strong, *The Exhaustive Concordance of The Bible*, Macdonald Publishing Company, Maclean, VA, 1890, p. 73.

W.E. Vine, Merrill F. Unger, William White, Jr., *Vine's Complete Expository Dictionary of Old and New Testament Words*, Thomas Nelson, Inc., Publishers, Nashville, TN, 1985, p. 438.

Ethelbert W. Bullinger, *A Critical Lexicon and Concordance to the English and Greek New Testament*, Zondervan Publishing House, Grand Rapids, MI, 1975, pp. 540, 541.

Joseph H. Thayer, *Thayer's Greek-English Lexicon of the New Testament*, Hendrickson Publishers, Inc., Peabody, MA, 1996, p. 610.

W.E. Vine, Merrill F. Unger, William White, Jr., *Vine's Complete Expository Dictionary of Old and New Testament Words*, Thomas Nelson, Inc., Publishers, Nashville, TN, 1985, p. 266.

Bernard A. Taylor, *The Analytical Lexicon to the Septuagint, A Complete Parsing Guide*, Zondervan Publishing House, Grand Rapids, MI, 1994, pp. 87, 414.

Sir Lancelot C.L. Brenton, *The Septuagint with Apocrypha: Greek and English*, Samuel Bagster & Sons, Ltd., London, 1851, p. 725.

Gerhard Kittel, *Theological Dictionary of the New Testament*, Wm. B. Eerdmans Publishing Company, Grand Rapids, MI, 1964, vol. 1, pp. 689–90.

James A. Brooks, Carlton L. Winbery, *Syntax of New Testament Greek*, University Press of America, Inc., Lanham, MD, 1979, p. 96.

A.T. Robertson, *A Grammar of the Greek New Testament in the Light of Historical Research*, Broadman Press, Nashville, TN, 1934, p. 889.

Ethelbert W. Bullinger, *A Critical Lexicon and Concordance to the English and Greek New Testament*, Zondervan Publishing House, Grand Rapids, MI, 1975, p. 125.

Joseph H. Thayer, *Thayer's Greek-English Lexicon of the New Testament*, Hendrickson Publishers, Inc., Peabody, MA, 1996, p. 279.

George V. Wigram, Ralph D. Winter, *The Word Study Concordance*, Tyndale House Publishers, Inc., Wheaton, IL, 1972, p. 43.

Joseph H. Thayer, *Thayer's Greek-English Lexicon of the New Testament*, Hendrickson Publishers, Inc., Peabody, MA, 1996, p. 39.

Wikipedia contributors. (2020, March 18). Non bis in idem. In Wikipedia, The Free Encyclopedia. Retrieved June 24, 2020 from https://en.wikipedia.org/w/index.php?title=Non_bis_in_idem&oldid=946239232.

Ethelbert W. Bullinger, *A Critical Lexicon and Concordance to the English and Greek New Testament*, Zondervan Publishing House, Grand Rapids, MI, 1975, p. 178.

Gerhard Kittel, *Theological Dictionary of the New Testament*, Wm. B. Eerdmans Publishing Company, Grand Rapids, MI, 1972, vol. 8, p. 399.

Ethelbert W. Bullinger, *A Critical Lexicon and Concordance to the English and Greek New Testament*, Zondervan Publishing House, Grand Rapids, MI, 1975, p. 683.

George V. Wigram, Ralph D. Winter, *The Word Study Concordance*, Tyndale House Publishers, Inc., Wheaton, IL, 1972, p. 163.

Ibid, p. 772.

David Alan Black, *It's Still Greek to Me: An Easy-to-Understand Guide to Intermediate Greek*, Baker Books, Grand Rapids, MI, 1998, p. 49.

Ethelbert W. Bullinger, *The Companion Bible*, Zondervan Bible Publishers, Grand Rapids MI, 1964, p. 1,661.

Adam Clarke Commentaries, "Instead of ἱερέων, priests, a few MSS., and the Syriac, read Ιουδαιων, Jews" [Judeans]. Retrieved May 18, 2020 from https://www. studylight.org/commentaries/acc/acts-6.html.

George V. Wigram, Ralph D. Winter, *The Word Study Concordance*, Tyndale House Publishers, Inc., Wheaton, IL, 1972, p. 772.

Ibid, p. 629.

The Zondervan Parallel New Testament in Greek and English, Zondervan Bible Publishers, Grand Rapids, MI, 1975, p. 361.

Harold K. Moulton, *The Analytical Greek Lexicon Revised*, Zondervan Publishing House, Grand Rapids, MI, 1978, p. 190.

Gerhard Kittel, *Theological Dictionary of the New Testament*, Wm. B. Eerdmans Publishing Company, Grand Rapids, MI, 1972, vol. 8, p. 518.

Joseph H. Thayer, *Thayer's Greek-English Lexicon of the New Testament*, Hendrickson Publishers, Inc., Peabody, MA, 1996, p. 84.

George Ricker Berry, *The Interlinear Literal Translation of the Greek New Testament*, Zondervan Publishing House, Grand Rapids, MI, 1979, p. 328.

Harold K. Moulton, *The Analytical Greek Lexicon Revised*, Zondervan Publishing House, Grand Rapids, MI, 1978, pp. 163, 190, 416.

A.T. Robertson, *A Grammar of the Greek New Testament in the Light of Historical Research*, Broadman Press, Nashville, TN, 1934, p. 882.

Ethelbert W. Bullinger, *The Companion Bible*, Zondervan Bible Publishers, Grand Rapids MI, 1964, Appendix 6, p. 12.

Barbara Friberg, Timothy Friberg, *Analytical Greek New Testament*, Baker Book House, Grand Rapids, MI, 1981, p. 728.

Ethelbert W. Bullinger, *A Critical Lexicon and Concordance to the English and Greek New Testament*, Zondervan Publishing House, Grand Rapids, MI, 1975, p. 596.

Ibid, p. 187.

Ibid., p. 812.

INDEX OF BIBLE REFERENCES

INDEX OF TERMS

Adam, 76, 112n20, 136-137

Age of Grace, 40, 77, 109, 151, 161, 171

"all things common," 67-68, 108

ambition, personal, 61

anakrinō (to judge again), 143

Ananias and Sapphira, 71-72, 74

Andersen, Hans Christian, 20

"another gospel," 32-34

apologeomai (answered), xv

apologia (to make one's defense), xv

authority

  centralization of, 46

  concentration of, 7

  and Christian leaders, xv, xviii, 7, 14, 17, 129, 154

  and God, xv, 14, 17-18, 46-47, 116, 129, 149-150

  and higher powers, 17-18

  and Jesus Christ, xv, 4, 16-17, 116, 149-150, 154

  speak truth to, 116, 165

auxanō (increased), 153

believe in God v. believe God, 99-100, 111-112, 125, 138-140

biblical behavior, 6-8, 46-47, 95, 99

Body of Christ

  building up of (edifying), 8, 42-44, 95-96

  Christ the head, 8, 44-45, 109, 149

  and equality (in importance), 112, 131, 159

  function in, 18, 18n4, 42, 45, 79, 95, 109, 112, 159, 168

idolatry, 7
institutional structures, xiv, 74,
    101, 113
intervention, 10, 107-108, 134
James, 38
Jefferson, Thomas, 10
Jesus (the man), 76
Jesus Christ
    accomplished work of, xviii, 10,
        23, 37, 53, 60-61, 76, 79, 83,
        93. 97, 100, 102, 104-105,
        109, 117, 126-127, 131, 136,
        142, 153, 158, 167-168, 171
    ascension of, 42, 52, 56, 86,
        92, 129-130
    Christ (the title and position),
        76, 149
    crucifixion of, 57, 111-112,
        129, 136-137, 144, 155
    as embodiment of man's
        spiritual life and future, 76,
        90, 92-93, 105, 112, 170-
        171
    as the embodiment of God's
        will and Word, xiii-xiv, xvi,
        xix, 3, 7, 10, 20, 28-30, 33,
        35, 37, 39-41, 45-47, 59,
        61-63, 65, 67, 72, 82, 84,
        90, 92-93, 99-101, 103-104,
        113, 116-119, 123-124, 126,

137, 152, 155, 157, 159,
    161, 167, 169-170
as example of service, xiii-xiv,
    xviii-xix, 1-5, 7, 9-10, 9n2,
    12-17, 15n3, 20, 43, 58, 62,
    84, 88, 90, 92-93, 96, 100,
    122
faith of, xv, xix, 9-10, 9n2, 12,
    29-30, 37, 59n13, 73, 81, 83,
    93, 97, 100-101, 103, 108-
    113, 117, 119, 122-123, 126,
    130-131, 137-141, 143-144,
    148-151, 154, 159, 161-162,
    167-168
and forgiveness, 35, 44, 123-
    124, 129, 158
as foundation, xiv, xviii, 12, 51,
    65, 75, 78, 80, 86, 94, 108-
    110, 126-127, 130, 139, 142,
    148, 150-151, 161, 167-168,
    170
as fulfillment of the law, 40,
    112, 140
at God's right hand, 100, 129,
    146, 149, 158
and good (representing all that
    is), 46
and gospel of grace, xiii
and greater works than, 101,
    131

service
  and Body of Christ, 7-8, 18,
    42-44, 95-96, 101, 109, 126,
    132, 159
  and business, xiv, 7, 96, 98,
    101-102, 159
  and Christ, 4- 9, 12-15, 17, 20,
    75, 88-94, 96-97, 99-101,
    109, 125-126, 136, 147, 159,
    167, 169-170
  Christ-centered, 75, 88, 109,
    125, 167, 169
  defined, 89, 91, 93-96, 98
  foundation of, xiv, 12, 75, 78,
    85, 91-98, 109, 126, 167,
    170
  and free will, 2
  and gifts to the church, 18-19,
    43, 95
  and God's Word, xiv, 3, 7, 20,
    33, 42-44, 42n7, 66-67, 75,
    84-85, 88, 90, 92-95, 98-
    102, 125-126, 136, 156, 159,
    166-167, 169-170
  and household of faith, xix, 8,
    44, 97-98, 100-102, 109,
    125-126, 159, 167
  and leadership, xiv, 2-4, 9, 12-
    13, 15, 18, 75, 95
  and life-giving purpose,
    satisfaction, and strength, 96

and Martha and Mary, 88-91,
  99, 101, 169-170
and positions of, 2-3, 18-20,
  42, 96
as remedy to lording over
  people, xix, 2-3, 9, 12, 14-15,
  17, 20
self-centered (or self-absorbed,
  self-serving), 88-90, 167,
  169-170
selfless, 14, 84, 88, 169
  and rewards, 14, 17, 85
seven, significance of, 78
sharing, xv, 10, 28-30, 35, 37,
  60-61, 68-70, 72, 97n15, 103,
  108, 117, 119, 125-126, 133,
  150, 172
shepherds, 16-17
sin nature, 136-137
speaking in tongues, 56-57, 59,
  130, 130n23
speaking up
  and fear, 20-21, 34
  and leaders lording over people,
    xvii, 19-20, 47, 122
  and perversions of God's Word,
    32-33, 114-115, 118
spirit of bondage, 146
spiritual attacks, xviii-xix, 21, 65,
  74

78, 85-86, 89, 93, 96-97, 103,
105, 112, 130, 133-134, 136-
137, 145-148, 150, 153-154,
157, 162, 168

"weak, the, (in the faith)," 83-84

will of God

and *homothumadon*, 84

leader's resistance to, xiv, xviii,
19, 128, 164, 168

prove it to yourself, 23-24, 47

winning people to Christ, 11-12,
160, 165

Word-based decisions, 1, 6, 8,
21, 24, 32, 34, 36, 43, 55n10,
63-64, 68, 92, 94, 105-106,
116-117, 125, 128, 135, 137,
139, 144, 147-148, 164-165

Word-centered dialogue, 32, 34,
107

Word-centered prayer, 28, 37, 47,
50, 52, 61, 66-67, 70-71, 86,
91, 93, 98, 101, 104, 125, 130-
131, 131n23, 134, 156-157

working with people where they
are, 1, 12-14, 34

works of men, 26, 35, 161, 167-
168

works of the law, 40, 60, 103,
111, 139

worldly things, xiv, 3-5, 7, 25, 51,
63, 82, 101, 128, 141, 143-
145, 164-165, 168, 171

A free ebook edition is available with the purchase of this book.

To claim your free ebook edition:

Visit MorganJamesBOGO.com
Sign your name CLEARLY in the space
Complete the form and submit a photo of
the entire copyright page
You or your friend can download the ebook
to your preferred device

Print & Digital Together Forever.

Snap a photo

Free ebook

Read anywhere

CPSIA information can be obtained
at www.ICGtesting.com
Printed in the USA
JSHW050955020422
24531JS00001B/18